Famous all over the world!

...ou INVEST in an AUSTIN

New Brakes. An improved type of braking system is employed, with individual cone adjustment at each wheel. Operation is by cam and plunger and is smooth and powerful.

New Clutch. A new type of clutch is fitted. The single centre plate carries the two friction rings, which are held apart by leaf springs so that power take-up is exceptionally smooth. Pedal operation is lighter.

For Safety. The new engine gives better performance, the new clutch easier engagement, and the new brakes more positive deceleration.

Other safety features are synchromesh engagement for second, third and top gears, automatic return direction indicators, Triplex toughened glass in windscreen, side and rear windows (except the Cabriolet rear window), *sun visor, remote control for the rear blind, dip-and-switch headlamp control, driving mirror, draught and fume excluders and ventilators.

For Economy. Over forty miles to the gallon of fuel is the normal average of the *Austin "Seven."* Tax and insurance are correspondingly light and other expenses are also on a strict economy basis. At less than a penny a mile for running costs, the *Austin "Seven"* remains the world's most economical motor car. It is easy to buy, easy to maintain, safe to drive, comfortable and dependable.

* Not on Fixed Head Saloon.

AMCO publication 1447E c July 1936.

A7CA archivist collection.

COLEMAN'S CARS

My Life with Motor Cars

Books by the same author:

Coleman's Drive Faber and Faber and NEP

Your Book of Veteran and Edwardian Cars Faber and Faber

Your Book of Vintage Cars Faber and Faber

Your Book of Racing Cars Faber and Faber

(These three books are due to be republished shortly as a single book with the title, A Short History of the Motor Car)

Childscourt Macdonald and NEP

Conscience of Europe Council of Europe Publishing

Froude Today NEP

COLEMAN'S CARS

My Life with Motor Cars

John Coleman

Published in the United Kingdom in 2008 by

European Atlantic Publications in association with
New European Publications Limited
14-16 Carroun Road
London SW8 1JT, England

British Library Cataloguing in Publication Data

ISBN 978 190 5770 205

Printed and bound in Great Britain by Antony Rowe Limited in Chippenham, Wiltshire.

Contents

Acknowledgements

My thanks to the many people in the vintage and classic car fraternity who, consciously or unconsciously, have contributed to this book and at the head of the former must be Dr Ian Mason-Smith, a retired senior scientist at the MoD researching into the British space programme and secretary of the Dorset Austin Seven Club, who undertook the editing of this book. Many good suggestions about the structure of the book originated in response to his first reading of it. He suggested and wrote the short summaries at the beginnings of the chapters. But most of all was the encouragement that followed my talk to the Dorset Austin Seven Club. Val Biro, whose wonderful books about Gumdrop must have influenced generations of children in sound directions, undertook to provide the foreword in his own inimitable way. I must mention Barrie Carter who persuaded me to have the Drive republished and who asked me to write an article about things on the journey that were not in the book, and somehow from that most of the other chapters seemed to spring into existence almost automatically.

I must thank Justin Glass, the managing director of European-Atlantic Publication, for his enormous encouragement, as well as Lloyd Allen who typeset the book and with whom I have long shared an interest in motor cars.

John Coleman 2008

Foreword

There is, undoubtedly, a close association between man and his vehicle of locomotion, a symbiosis, and there always has been. Just look at with what devotion Noah built his Ark with so many cubits of gopher wood planks, and how enthusiastically Caractacus drove his chariot into the invading Roman hordes; not to speak of the 18C young blade in his curricle, powered by thoroughbred "cattle", or certainly of Gottlieb Daimler and his first horseless carriage. (And when I say "man", I use the term advisedly, for it is a truth universally acknowledged that for a woman a vehicle is no more than a means of transport.)

For us males, however, it is rather more. How many of us, when young, have stood at the kerbside, enumerating, identifying, categorising and admiring the cars – and cars were proper cars then – which went roaring past; or permitted, sat in the driving seat and holding those lovely, big, fat steering wheels, pretending to drive, even if our short-trousered legs weren't yet able to reach the pedals? There is something of Toad in most of us, about cars. Look at how Kenneth Grahame describes Toad's first encounter with the motor car, as he walks with Rattie behind his horsedrawn caravan:

> "Far behind them, they heard a faint warning hum, like the drone of a distant bee. Glancing back, they saw a small cloud of dust, with a dark centre of energy, advancing on them at incredible

speed… when in an instant (as it seemed)… it was on them! The "poop-poop" rang with a brazen shout in their ears, they had a moment's glimpse of an interior of glittering plate-glass and rich morocco, and the magnificent motor-car, immense, breath-snatching, passionate, with its pilot tense and hugging his wheel, possessed all earth and air for the fraction of a second… and then dwindled to a speck in the far distance, changed back into a droning bee once more."

This – one of the finest paragraphs in all English Literature, I submit – so well describes our feelings at first sight of a car. (It was true of me when, in later years, I came to write my 36 children's books about a car called Gumdrop, which – "breath-snatching, passionate" – I still drive around to this day.)

And it must certainly be true of John Coleman, who describes in this delightful book his relationship with the many cars he has known since a child. He writes about them with enthusiasm, cheerfulness, knowledge, and humour – qualities which must have been handy on his epic drive – in a 1925 Austin 7 Chummy – from Argentina to New York. Whether he praises or criticises the many cars he has known or driven, he does so with affection and empathy, which make this book an essential *vade mecum* for all car enthusiasts and true descendants of the immortal Mr Toad.

Val Biro

Chapter 1

Childhood and Motor Cars

The motor car is now Public Enemy Number One but perhaps that is not quite right. Perhaps the jet airliner beats it by a small margin, emitting vast clouds of pollution into the upper atmosphere, but it is into the upper atmosphere and that is not so immediate and we do not feel it so directly. After a short time the omnipresent motor car hits us where it really hurts, in our own locality, and something would have been done about it long ago if most of the trouble were not in somebody else's backyard. So the question is: need it have been so? In 1905 Stenson Cooke, the first Secretary of the A.A. wrote his magnificent little book, *This Motoring*, in which he hoped a rational government would undo the harm done by the railways – he hoped! The old staging inns of rural and small-town urban England would come to life again. After all the railways were like a large system of by-passes, or perhaps more accurately, motorways. By the middle of the Victorian era people in the main travelled from one of the great industrial cities to another and bypassed the smaller towns in between, which comprised the greater part of the character of old England. When they did stop it was at the rather standard, boring railway hotels. There was a synergy (one of the horrible words we use today) between the old market towns and the surrounding countryside. The railways took a lot of it away by rushing fresh fruit and vegetables into the big cities. The people of those old cities – London was once thought of as a collection of villages in the days when Wordsworth could survey it from Westminster Bridge – clung to many of their old ways. In the northern industrial towns they had the 'village' stores pretty nearly at the end of every street.

Ah, yes, and when did it all go awry? I believe that it did so when the idea of 'motoring for the millions' took root in the popular imagination. To begin with motor manufacturers built their cars in their own back yards and then in slightly better sheds and workshops, and firms who made other things such as bicycles and sowing machines started to turn towards the seductive vision of motor cars. Henry Ford of course led the way. Others followed. For some time just before and just after the First World War, production in Europe was mainly in the hands of individual people and a few individuals working for them. Small was quite fascinating and really rather beautiful. Two sorts of person wanted motor cars: the rich who could afford them and for whom the car was really a sort of toy and the technically minded who stretched their resources to get anything on four wheels. Both wanted the motor car for fun and that was OK. Val Biro reflects it in his story of Gumdrop, an Austin Heavy 12/4: 'Mr Josiah Oldcastle was a vintage car enthusiast. Which was not surprising, because he had a vintage car of his own, called Gumdrop. He loved driving the old car just for fun...' It was when the motor car became useful that the trouble started. I shall say more about that in the chapter, 'The Terrible Mistake'. Mass production, which had started with Ford in America, was beginning in England in the second half of the nineteen-twenties, prices were slashed and greedy manufacturers began to monopolise the market, buying up their component suppliers to deprive their rivals of successful parts, such as SU carburettors. Not much free trade there!

I do not remember the twenties. It was not until the beginning of the thirties that I first became conscious of motor cars as such. My father had trained at Vickers and it was only recently that I found the certificate they sent to the War Office claiming that his designing work was vital to the war effort. I think that like my uncle he had wanted to join the Royal Flying Corps but had some slight trouble with his eyesight. At any rate he was up to his eyebrows in machinery. I knew when I was very small indeed that he had a number of motorbikes. It must have been in the family because each of his four sisters had one. There is one story that cropped up regularly. The family was living in Woolwich at the time and my father had gone to fetch my favourite aunt from somewhere in Kent on one of the old belt driven motorbikes. In order to get up hills in those days you had to race like mad as you approached them. My aunt was on the pillion when they left but as they came to, I think it was Shooters Hill, he gave it full throttle and just managed to get up without any slip and arrived home in triumph, except that there was no one behind him. I don't think my aunt could have been badly hurt because the story always caused much laughter in the family and he never heard the end of it.

My own first dim memory was of being carried by my mother in a side car which he had fitted to one of his motorbikes, but as I got a little bigger I remember we got an AC with a Dickey seat. The front seat was of the bench type and I used to sit in the middle and was told what a wonderful car it was. I now know that was absolutely right and I wouldn't mind having it today. Unfortunately I was the cause of having to make a change. I gradually got too big to fit comfortably in the middle. At any rate it was a good car to make my first acquaintance in this world with the motor car. I don't remember ever being uncomfortable in it but I have a ghastly recollection of sitting in the back of the cars that followed and being desperately sick in all of them almost until the time when I drove myself. The first car that came after the AC was a Swift. I recall that my father liked it enormously and was always very positive about it. I was not old enough then to appreciate its technical significance but I do remember one curious feature about it. The seats could be manoeuvred to make a double bed. The only problem with that was that it took up all the space in the car and there was no room left for anything else. It was the cause of endless discussion but I never remember it being used. It was more of a fantasy than a practical reality. The next car was a Rover. My father hated it and pronounced it to be rubbish in spite of the reputation it was supposed to have acquired. He was rather definite on matters of this sort. At the time he was working for Sir Geoffrey de Havilland, whom he both liked and greatly admired. He'd been working for Handley Page earlier and he used to say that he should go back to his furniture removing. He had a similar view of William Morris. I suppose he would have said he should have returned to his bicycle shop, or perhaps never have left it. My father also thought pre-war Morrises heavy and cumbersome, although he liked the Morris Minor when it came out in 1948. Herbert Austin was the man he really admired and he often talked of the Austin Seven Swallow in glowing terms though we never had one.

By the time war came in 1939, millions were motoring, driving tests had only fairly recently been introduced and only twenty or so years earlier horse buses were the normal way of travel in London. My father remembered them well as a boy and the man on the Clapham omnibus was almost certainly horse drawn. It is desperately hard to believe that things which were there at the beginning of our lives have not been there for ever. To those who were young when I was a small child the motor car, like the aeroplane, seemed an amazingly new thing. The war, of course, brought the development of the car to an abrupt halt and every effort was turned towards perfecting machines for the war, that would outdo the enemy on land, sea and in the air, most famously the Spitfire. My father turned to an Austin Seven to get the miles per gallon. He had a small ration for the work that he was doing and I think occasionally added a little paraffin when things were desperate, but it was a serious offence to do so and the police stopped you if there were signs of black smoke coming from your exhaust.

I caught scarlet fever at the end of 1939 and so after a brief spell of being evacuated I was brought back home. Nothing seemed to be happening and I was glad to be at home to recover. It was a tense time. I listened to Churchill's speech on the radio and we all knew we could be invaded at any moment. I was thankful to be with my family. Motor cars played a negligible part in my life at that ghastly stage. My father sometimes used his car in connection with his work but that was all. Then in August 1940 everything changed. The Luftwaffe attacked Croydon. I could hear the anti-aircraft guns a few miles away and I went out on to the balcony and could see the explosions near the German bombers. It didn't quite seem real – yet. If the sirens went now we went down into a reinforced basement room with sandbags at the windows. On the following Saturday afternoon after the warning had gone we were sitting there with friends including a young soldier who had been at the front in France at the start of the war. The bombs showered down that afternoon. Three landed within a hundred yards or so of our house. The prospect seemed serious. I was twelve at the time. The soldier said it was worse than being at the front. You had to sit and wait for the bombs to fall on you. At the front at least you felt you could do something about it. His remarks impressed themselves on my mind and I've never forgotten them. I was put to sleep under an old Victorian dresser that was built into one side of the room and I felt pretty safe. It was like that for about a week and the bombing got pretty heavy.

One night my father came home and my parents had decided that we must leave London. We picked up a friend and her elderly mother and set off hoping to get out of London before the raids started, but it was not to be. As we reached Dulwich the raid started and our passengers became very nervous. At the top of Denmark Hill there was one of those brick surface shelters which were fine for saving you from broken glass and minor

explosions but not much more. My mother and father decided
we should get out of London as fast as possible. Our friends
refused to leave the shelter so we set out on what was without
doubt the most memorable car journey ever for me, including
the whole of my South American trip. The fireworks started and
on a couple of occasions we came up against fresh bomb craters
in the road and had to turn round and make our way through
the side streets to get back again on the main road. My father
drove as fast as he could through the blacked-out streets with
masked headlights with only three little slits for a glimmer of
light to get through. However the ack-ack fire and the bombs
provided frequent flashes of light and we reached somewhere
near Slough when a German aircraft swooped down and started
machine gunning the road. My father quickly pulled off the
road, stopped under a tree and switched the lights off completely and waited until the danger seemed to have passed over. The
rest of the journey to High Wycombe was uneventful.

We arrived in the dark, very early hours of the morning and
as far as I remember had a brief sleep before venturing out to
look for the first signs of life. We knew that German bombers
could not reach this far and we were safe. I could see that my
mother had tears in her eyes as we drove into the centre of town
where we found a café that opened at six o'clock for bus drivers
coming to work. I don't remember whether we had anything to
eat but I suppose we did. Much more important we started to
talk to one of the drivers and told him of our plight. My father
had to return to Croydon as soon as possible, so it was an
immense relief when he said to my father: 'Take your wife and
your boy to my home and my wife will look after them until you
find somewhere to stay'. He wrote a little note and they were as
good as, if not better than their word. My father drove straight
back to Croydon after leaving us in the care of the kind bus
driver's wife. Every nook and cranny in High Wycombe was
filled with people fleeing from London and there was simply no
where to stay. Hotels were crammed full and the idea of finding

anywhere to rent was out of the question. My mother, who was always exceptionally good at dealing with authorities, searched for weeks and eventually went to the town clerk, who not surprisingly said that he had nothing he could possibly offer her, but in the end mentioned that he had one derelict, condemned cottage on the end of a row beside a stream. It had no running water, no bathroom, no electricity and was very damp. My mother said straightaway, 'We'll have it.'

It was all he said and worse. The toilet was a bucket in a shed in the garden and nearly all the windows were broken. My mother found someone to mend them and lit blazing fires in the two downstairs rooms to dry the place out. The following weekend my father brought my grandfather and my favourite aunt as well as a very good water filter to stand beside the pump at the old grey stone sink and a couple of Aladdin lamps with mantles which gave out a beautiful, gentle light. My mother and my aunt painted and decorated the place themselves. It was called No 1 Marsh Cottages and if the cottage had everything wrong with it, the garden had everything right. Things grew almost like Jack's bean. I dug for victory and I kept chickens, also for victory I thought, and went to a little local private school where I was very happy. One Sunday afternoon the headmistress and her husband walked past and apparently saw me building a chicken house. The next day in lessons she came over to me and said, 'I wish you'd work at your Latin in the way you were working at that chicken house yesterday.'

Now if you were to think that all this has nothing to do with motor cars, you'd be wrong. During the winter the raids on London died down and had stopped altogether for at least a couple of months. My father came down for weekends, often by train to save petrol, but this time he had the car and was going to take my mother up for the day to get some things and see the house. I badgered them to take me with them and reluctantly they agreed. There was a large sheet of glass which I wanted very badly for a frame in the garden, and lots of things in my bedroom upstairs I wanted to check were safe. I knew the house had been hit by an incendiary oil bomb a couple of days after we'd left which fortunately didn't ignite, though the core of it went straight through the dresser under which I'd slept. I wouldn't have stood much chance if I'd been there. I was really keen to see it. As we approached London on a bright Sunday morning a heavy pall of smoke hung over the city with a red glow to it. It was clear that something was wrong. We soon learned that there had been a heavy and unexpected raid during the night. The days were safe or so we thought, and we went on in to town. I saw that my things were largely unharmed and persuaded my father fix the three foot square sheet of glass securely on the back of the car, a considerable feat indeed. Other things were packed inside the car and I squeezed in beside them. I think we all felt fairly content with our visit, but we didn't like the thought that the raids had started again. My mother had wanted to see the house but we didn't hang about for too long. We were driving out towards the A40 and approaching the railway bridge over the road just before the Lambeth crossing of the Thames where a cyclist cut in front of us and my father cursed him, little knowing the good turn he may have done us. We went under the bridge where a policeman immediately in front stopped us when suddenly the loudest bang I have ever heard seemed to stun the whole world. The policeman went straight upwards. A great iron girder came down diagonally across the windscreen and almost on to the bonnet. A time bomb from the previous night had exploded on top of the bridge and engulfed everything in front of us in a cloud of smoke. When the smoke had subsided we saw a way through by going partly on the pavement. My parents tried to divert my attention but I saw briefly what I knew must be the remains of the policeman on the right-hand side of the road. There was nothing we could do and we had to get out of London as rapidly as possible.

Motor cars didn't really come into the picture for the rest of the war. My aunt and my grandfather found a dilapidated bungalow but also a builder to repair it. I developed bronchitis and a year later we moved to Kent on doctor's orders to get over it and then I went away to boarding school. When I was at home I was more interested in my bike and in recognising the aeroplanes I occasionally saw in dog fights in the sky above me than in motor cars. What a mad time it was! My father had a favourite story which he often repeated whenever the occasion permitted: a bomb fell on a lunatic asylum and all the lunatics came running out waving their arms and shouting, 'Who are the lunatics now?' I never knew how authentic it was, but it surely enshrines a fundamental truth.

Chapter 2

On My Own Wheels

The next phase in my life took me right away from motor cars. I was at boarding school in Hertfordshire and occasional doodlebugs and even a V2 rocket, which fell on the football field, made a much bigger impact than motor cars, which hardly seemed to exist for some years and were largely up on blocks in locked-up garages. The war in Europe ended in 1945 and at the beginning of term one of the boys used to boast about how he had driven his father's car down from London in a fantastically short time. Of course we didn't even believe that his father had let him drive, never mind the tall stories about time. I thought no more about it until some years later an old school friend told me that the boy was gaining quite a reputation in motor racing. He was Stirling Moss. After leaving school I went back to live at home in London and started a degree course at King's College. Suddenly one morning at the end of the first term my call-up papers came through the letter box and as a result I was faced with a choice whether to apply for postponement on educational grounds or to go ahead and get my National Service over, a choice incidentally that was to have a huge effect on my life with motor cars, although I didn't realize it at the time. A new era of motoring was about to begin and curiously that term at university was to play a key part. The only immediate experience I had at home then was that a new friend, Dick Thomas, who had been at Dulwich College, had one of the original Morris Minor tourers, from 1931 and 8 horsepower, in which he used to collect his friends to play tennis on the courts at Peckham Rye. I used to look down at it sometimes from my window at the top of our house. It was an amazing sight, as many as twelve piled high in the back of the poor little car. When Dick called for you it was not to get in, but to pile on, the car – and you did exactly that to the squeals and yells and laughs of those underneath. It all seemed a great deal of fun and I remember once in a small private road, when the tennis contingent were not present, Dick suggested that I should have a go at driving the car. I can't recall whether I did actually drive it or whether the thought was so vivid that I now believe I did. Somehow that car sparked a new interest in motoring although I was not in a position to do anything about it at the time with conscription looming.

Anyway the fatal day arrived, 16th January 1947, and I was ordered to report to the barracks at Devizies in Wiltshire. I duly did so and was given a uniform that more or less fitted me and was marched into a real old English Army barracks, up a couple of flights of stone steps severely worn by soldiers boots for a hundred or more years, and into the barest barrack room possible to imagine: old bare boards provided a floor, equally bare walls enclosed it and two long rows of iron beds that slotted into half their size in the daytime with three 'biscuits', small square mattresses, carefully piled up with two or three blankets neatly folded on top. At night you extended the beds to their full length to make just about the most uncomfortable beds con-ceivable – short of a bed of nails. The ordinary soldier today has a lot to thank Field Marshal Montgomery for. He changed all that and introduced comfortable beds with bedside lamps to boot.

Anyway that is not to the point although a little more of my army experience is necessary to the story because of the big part that service was to play in my introduction to motoring. I won't

mention what it was like to be out on Salisbury Plain in army
huts with leaking roofs and no fuel in the worst winter of the
20th century. We went to bed in our great coats. The next stage
in my military existence also didn't quite involve the motor car
but certainly led the way to it. I found myself posted to the Royal
Signals in Catterick where I learnt one of the most useful skills
the army offered me, without which there's a good chance that
this book wouldn't have been written; I learnt to type. However
I don't think my skills in this direction were greatly appreciated
by the army. The ATS girls did a far better job than I could ever
have managed, especially on the big old teleprinters. The other
good thing that happened to me at Catterick was to get on to the
Regimental Cross Country Running team, as I had done some
cross country running at school. It was quite amazing how I
could avoid unpleasant chores by showing what they called a
'chit' with 'Regimental Team' on it. I never quite realized at the
time that the preparation for those runs might stand me in good
stead for the much longer 'run' later in my life.

I had tried during my Primary Training to become an
Education Corps (later Royal) Sergeant but I had made the
mistake of mentioning to the Personal Selection Officer (PSO)
that I had inclinations towards being a conscientious objector
and, although I had great conversations with him about war and
felt he was more or less on my side, he explained that he could
not recommend me for the Education Corps, since in the event
of another war the AEC automatically became an infantry corps.
He thought I would be far better off getting through my
National Service in the Royal Signals and that certainly seemed
to be the best course.

I had hesitated about applying for a commission as I thought
it would involve an extra year or so added to my 'time', and I certainly didn't want that. However, when I got to Catterick I was
told I could apply without signing up for more than the basic
two years. So I did. I had become friendly with one of the clerks
in the Company office and he mentioned to me that there were

two trays, one for those going straight to WOSB (War Office Selection Board) and one for those going to pre-OCTU (which was a pretty harsh spell of training and drilling) before their WOSB. 'I could slip your application, which has been passed, over into the direct tray, if you like' he said. The temptation was too great and in any case I'd had more than my full share of training at a special course at Chester and with the Signals. Surely I deserved some benefit from that. The result was positive and almost immediate. Before I knew where I was I was at the WOSB. We were treated like gentlemen. We sat down to fine dinners, served in style, and given hell. We went round battle courses and goodness knows what, but the best part for me was when we were set practical tasks in teams, such as getting a lorry chassis over a ten-foot wall. Each member of the team had a turn as leader, and if he didn't succeed within a certain time the others could volunteer to take over. Well, these were exactly the kind of practical challenges I loved to deal with. I took over five out of the six tasks and I felt quite sure I'd created a pretty good impression. I was to learn later that they were in principle very similar to the kind of challenges that old motor cars faced you with. Next came the IQ tests. I'd always disliked using my thinking processes in an abstract way but on that occasion it may have been a relief after a surfeit of practical stuff and I was later told that my results were pretty good. Perhaps a kind of inspiration was carried over from those earlier practical tasks. However the *piece de resistance* – I can't describe it adequately without using a few French words – came at the end. A General came to give the final interview at the end of the three gruelling days. I was sitting outside waiting, a little nervous but feeling pretty sure that on the whole it had been the kind of testing situation I liked and enjoyed, when a young soldier came out of the interview room. I couldn't believe my eyes. He was an old school friend of mine. So I said, 'What on earth are you doing here?' 'I've just been in to see my dad. He's the General for this batch,' he explained and slipped back in to see his father.

The outcome of all this was that I got an immediate commission in the Army Education Corps, and, unlike the Sergeants, the officers did not become part of the infantry but could get into special services such as Intelligence in the event of war. I returned to Catterick to wait for a week or so before the results came in and in that time I managed to get a 48 hour pass and of course went down to London. Earlier I had been chosen for the Royal Signals' cross country running team and I was usually able to use this as an excuse to get off duty early, especially for weekend leaves. As a result of doing so on this occasion an event occurred which had nothing to do with motor cars, but was sufficient to prevent me becoming swollen headed after the success of the WOSB.

At school I had gained the War Office Certificate A, something that almost everybody in the Corps managed to get but I had been somewhat lazy about it and the others in my House got pretty angry with me. I was letting the House down. The great test was in the afternoon and a contingent of officers had arrived down from the War Office. It was also coming up towards the time for School Certificate, and we were given the morning for revision. However, the looming ordeal of that very afternoon pressed much more heavily on my mind and I took my army manual with me into the classroom and set about getting at least a few of the main platoon arrangements into my head. I even marked the pages. The afternoon arrived and we went through the usual drill and exercises and the time came for individual questions. It was my turn and I was asked some rather tricky questions about a platoon with a Bren gun. I gave my answer to the Major who was examining me. 'I'm afraid you're wrong,' he said, and with uncharacteristic boldness, I replied, 'I don't think I am wrong, Sir.' To which he retorted rather sharply, 'I'm afraid you are.' I then said I was very surprised. At that point he got out the army manual to show me. He fumbled slightly over the pages. 'You'll find it on page 72 (or whatever it was), Sir'. It was on 72 and I was right. When the results were posted I came top for the whole school for that year and I got my Certificate A with flying colours much to the amazement of those who thought they were going to have to rough me up.

That qualification played it part in my military career. When I returned to Catterick I had a couple of weeks to wait before my immediate commission took effect so I applied successfully for a weekend pass and, of course, made my way down to London. Earlier I had failed my typing exam and was put in a platoon for the Barrier Failures, known as the BFs naturally! I wasn't too worried as I knew now that I wasn't in any case going to spend the rest of my army service banging away on a teleprinter. I'd learnt to type as well as I'd ever want for my own purposes. I'd been selected earlier, as I said, for the Royal Signals cross country running team and I had a 'chit', as we called it, just a little piece of paper signed by some senior officer, saying so, and it worked like magic when I wanted to get off duty early, especially for weekend leave. Any tendency to become swollen headed on account of my WOSB success was about to be severely shaken, if not completely shattered. Because I left early I had failed to read Friday's Company Orders. My Cert A had earned me one stripe and I became a Lance Corporal without knowing it. I pushed my leave to the limit and arrived back only a few minutes before 8 o'clock when the whole company was due to be on parade and I didn't know I was supposed to be the marker for the BF platoon. I thought I could just shuffle on to the end of the line and be unnoticed. I really bungled it and the Sergeant-Major roared out to the whole company 'We've got a real bloody fool on parade this morning' in a way that only the old British Army Sergeant-Majors could. I lost my stripe in double quick time.

My humiliation, however, was brief and within a few days I was called into the Commanding Officer who explained to me that I was still a Private while I was in the Signals but that as soon as I was outside the camp gates my commission applied and I was an Officer, 'Yes, sir, I understand,' I replied with considerable feeling of well-being and relief. 'You'll go out in an army truck to the station and I want you to put these two pips on your uniform and cover them up with these two pieces of khaki cloth which you can take off once you're outside the camp, and here's a rail ticket to Buchanan Castle in Scotland, the headquarters of the Army Education Corps, where you will have to report, and after that you can have a week's leave before reporting to Glen Parva barracks in Leicester.' It all sounded fine to me, but even at that stage it never crossed my mind that this new stage in my life would have anything to do with motor cars. Oh, I nearly forgot, I did a rather grand course on education at the Army Education Centre at Eltham Palace. Even the Secretary of State came down to speak to each course and every week we went up to the House of Commons and had a session listening to debates in Parliament.

In due course I went to Leicester to begin the real work. I had to report to the Colonel in charge of Education for North Midland District. The District General was very keen on Education and especially on helping young servicemen to prepare for civilian life. It was good and almost at once I felt that what I was doing was really worthwhile. I was now an Area Education Officer and had to visit and organize three major education centres as well as ensuring that all the army units in my area were providing effective education both on a general basis with regular lectures on British Way and Purpose (BWP) as well as trying to cater for the special needs of soldiers in the months before demobilisation. A lot of travelling was absolutely necessary and that was where the question of a car came in. To start off with I used army transport but the General decided to pay Area Officers very good allowances if they ran their own cars. All AEOs were offered this opportunity. Now for the first time having a car that was actually my own entered my head. For some years after the war very few new cars were being made and second-hand, pre-war cars were hugely expensive, unless they were very old indeed and hardly practical (the price range has now reversed). So on leave I discussed the situation with my father. The outcome was that my first car was a 1931 Singer 8. I don't remember what I paid for it nor where it came from. But I have a dim recollection of a yard with a number of old cars that had been stored there through the war and, as most of them had girder chasses from which the main body of the car could be detached, the thing to look for was a crack in the chassis or signs of a repair. If either of these was evident everyone said not to touch the car with a bargepole. In that respect the Singer was sound and it was my own, my very own first car. The prospect of using it, however, was fairly nerve racking and dampened the enthusiasm I might otherwise have had. My father drove me up to Leicester in it and returned to London by train. A suitable army shed was found for it and a Sergeant detailed to take me out and teach me to drive it. My excitement with my new toy didn't last long. On the first outing the splines on the shaft coming out of the gear box into the clutch sheared and I had scarcely attempted to drive the wretched machine. I had it repaired in a local garage and it was fine for a few miles and then the problem repeated itself. I thought at the time it was due to a fault in the alignment of the shaft, but perhaps that was just what the garage told me, although looking back now I suspect that the welding was not adequately hardened. At any rate I gave up the idea of learning on it and left it to rest indefinitely in the shed at the barracks.

A new approach to motoring was called for, I thought, so when I next went home on leave I told my father the sad story and asked for his advice. He thought the best thing was to go round to Jack Surtees, the father of John, who had a motorcycle shop in Stanstead Road, Forest Hill, to see if he knew of a suitable car. He was an absolutely trustworthy chap and wouldn't recommend anything he suspected to be unsound. The next very day he drove up to our front gate with a smart little dark blue 1935 Y Model Ford 8, that looked like the sort of car that would really suit me. I hadn't reckoned with the remarks that came later: 'Tin Lizzy,' and 'if you can't afford a car, buy a Ford.' Anyway £150 seemed a very fair price and one that I could scrape up with a little bit of help. We went for a drive in it and it seemed fine and lively, although my father never had any great liking for Fords. So we settled on it and once again my father had to drive it up to Leicester.

I was the proud owner of two cars now, although I didn't quite know what to do about the first one. A new era in my relationship with motor cars was dawning and I felt pretty privileged. Very few young men at the age of 19 owned a motor car in those days and here was I owning two! The Sergeant in the motor transport section was again detailed to teach me in the course of going round the education centres and units for which I was responsible. The Sergeant was a rather nervous young chap as I was myself. I learnt all the usual things: how to steer, how to change gear, how to brake and what to do in an emergency. I was aware of 'original sin' and a cruel streak in our natures but I don't think I quite realized what I was doing on the first day out, when I was just starting to drive with a burst of learner's over-confidence along the clear, empty, country roads. 'What do I do if I want to stop it?' I asked the poor Sergeant breezily. I now realize the agony he must have gone through during that week. By Wednesday I was driving in the City of Leicester itself and by Thursday I was able to arrange to take my driving test in Newark on Friday morning. My ambition was to have another weekend pass and drive the car down to London on Saturday. I made my visits to the centres and to the various army units brief and I was driving virtually from morning till night. On Friday morning I set out for Newark with the Sergeant. We reached the airfield just north of Newark on which the REME (Royal Electrical and Mechanical Engineers) unit was based, after driving through the centre of both towns for a bit of last minute practice. I was nervous, very nervous. The Motor Transport Officer was a pleasant man and directed the Sergeant to the Sergeants' mess where he could have a drink and stay for lunch. He then got into the car beside me and wisely took me out on to the runway to cover the basics. When he had satisfied himself that those basic techniques were more of less tolerable, he took me for a drive outside the camp and in light traffic, which was really a rather a gentle part of the test and certainly nothing like driving through the centre of Leicester. When we returned, however, I went slightly past the narrow lane, hardly more than a pathway, leading up to the Officers' Mess. 'Reverse up there to the Mess,' he said, 'and I'll pass you.' It was long, at least five or six hundred yards. Fortunately I didn't have time to contemplate how daunting it was, which was perhaps why I made it. Until then I had thought how lucky I was to take my test in the Army but that changed my mind. We had lunch and one small drink together and then went to the Company Office for him to fill in and sign the pink form, which was the Certificate of Competence to Drive and had to be taken to the local licensing office to get a civilian driving licence. I was feeling pretty elated. 'Tomorrow morning,' I thought to myself, 'I'll go to the licensing office, (they were local then), and fill up with petrol and be on my way to London' but disaster struck. The office was out of the pink forms and they couldn't get any more before the following week. However, the officer said, 'I'll write a letter on military paper and the MTO at any unit will sign one for you.' So I returned to Leicester with the Sergeant and found a unit that had one of the pink forms. I thought my troubles were over; I was to call in and get it the following morning. When I arrived at the unit, however, the pink form was there but the MTO had gone away for the weekend. I was getting desperate. 'There's only one thing for it,' I thought, 'I'll take the pink form and sign it myself and put the MTO's letter with it,' and that was what I did. When I got to the office no questions were asked and I duly received my driving licence. 'I've done it,' I thought, 'and I bet there are not many people who have signed their own Certificates of Competence to Drive.' But I did slightly wonder if someone would find out one day and create a rumpus. No one has and nearly sixty years have passed. But that was not what was worrying me that day. My mind was filled with the thought that I was going to give everyone at home a huge surprise. I revelled in the thought, although the knowledge that I had to drive right through central London slightly dampened my buoyant enthusiasm. I drove from Leicester to South London on Saturday and back again on Monday – I could squeeze in a little extra time at weekends and make it up during the week – and I was not disappointed at the response. My girl friend, Anne, wanted to visit Hatfield House but that had to wait till later.

The next week I managed to get myself transferred from Leicester to Newark. There was a much more relaxed attitude in the REME Officers' Mess than in the old traditional regiment and the messing charges were considerably lower. I told my Colonel at District HQ that it would help me to pay for my car and he completely understood. The Army like nothing else – except perhaps the other services though I couldn't say for certain about them – is an organisation where knowing the right people in the right places can work miracles. During the rest of that week I had the satisfying experience of travelling from unit to unit under my own steam, or rather, my own control. I'm sure the poor Sergeant who taught me so successfully must have been immensely relieved. I had not, however, yet developed the judgment of long motoring experience. Some minor scrapes I suppose were inevitable. Most I have forgotten but one impressed itself on my mind. I was taking another officer round with me who wanted to visit some of my units. He was an Irishman who prided himself on using his country's brand of humour. On the way I caught the chromium hub cap of my nearside front wheel on a protruding part of a car parked by the roadside and knocked it off – the hub cap that is, not the car! No damage was done. I picked up the hub cap and I suspect I learned a lesson: the need to give other objects on the road a reasonable berth. My colleague must have measured the potential for humour to be extracted from the incident and later, in conversation with the Commanding Officer of the unit, he says, 'Ah, to be sure we had a fine journey from Newark: only one small accident when a stationary car ran into him'. 'Hell,' I thought, 'I'm not going to give that blighter an opportunity to say anything like that again,' and the lesson I thought I had learned earlier was well and truly reinforced. Unfortunately there was worse to come, although it was something I then reckoned I could blame on fate and not on my own inaccurate stupidity.

Saturday arrived, the Saturday after my great trip to London and perhaps I was a little too flushed with success, despite the small incident of the hub cap. I decided to stay in the camp for the weekend as I felt that my sense of adventure had been more than adequately satisfied during the previous week. When Saturday evening came two of my fellow Second Lieutenants said, 'You've got a car. Let's have an evening out.' So I agreed, feeling somewhat at an advantage for being able to provide the transport. We changed into our 'civies' and prepared to see what Newark offered in the way of Saturday evening entertainment: a cinema, a dance, a drink or whatever. We all piled into my much appreciated Ford 8, but fate had something different in store for us from what we had anticipated. As we were going down the hill into town suddenly I saw a car wheel rolling down in front of me. It took a moment for me to realize that it was mine. And then there was a crash as the offside of the front axle hit the ground and an extended scraping noise as I instinctively put my foot on the brake pedal, trying to practice what I'd learned about emergency stops the previous week. In spite of my inexperience it seemed that the only thing to do was to get out and try to assess the damage. The front axle beam was badly bent, the wing was crumpled and the brake drum was cracked. I felt the whole car was useless. It was Saturday evening and there was no hope of getting help from the local garage and I hadn't yet got round to joining the AA which in those days meant an outlay of £2 a year and £2 then was real money. What were we to do? One of my companions went and brought the wheel back and I jacked the front of the car up, and we managed to fix it on roughly, having borrowed a couple of wheel nuts from the other wheels, and wobbled to the nearest garage which fortunately was at the bottom of the hill. We walked into town, had a drink or two and set out on foot to return to camp. On Monday morning the MTO found me some army transport so that I could continue my duties and call in at the garage on the way out. Later that week the estimate for repairs came in. The front axle had to come off and the axle beam straightened, the front wing repaired and resprayed, a new brake drum and various brake parts fitted, the chassis checked for possible distortion, the steering realigned and set and the inevitable bits and bobs, all of which items added up to the astronomical sum of just over £20. The work had to be done. I was lucky that the car could be saved at all and my Colonel was very kind and rubber stamped my slightly exaggerated mileage claims.

Another lesson had been learnt and learnt for the rest of my motoring life: always make sure that the wheel nuts are tight. Even now whenever I take a wheel off I put the hub cap or wheel cover on the ground nearby to put the nuts in and never put the caps back without a second check on the tightness of the nuts. If any unusual noises are coming from the car the first thing I do is to check that a wheel is not loose. After a week or so I got the car back and, somewhat sobered, I continued my motoring career, covering a very considerable mileage for the Army and supplementing my civilian ration with a generous army allowance and a car that did a remarkable mpg, enabling me to make fairly regular trips back home to London. Various incidents, of course, occurred. One such was when I stopped on the roadside as I was returning to the unit at Retford. I pulled the button to start up. The engine seemed to be locked solid. 'It's seized,' was the inexperienced thought that flew through my mind. 'My God,' I thought, 'this motoring really is one damn thing after another.' By that time, however, I had overstretched my resources to join the AA, and, although you got an hour's work done by the roadside free, I feared that this was going to involve another crippling £20 bill for a reconditioned engine. Anyway the immediate thing was to find the nearest phone box, which I did. The result was that a mechanic from a nearby garage arrived in a remarkably short time, before catastrophic visions of the future had an opportunity to upset my mental balance. I briefly described the symptoms. He jumped into the car, put it into second gear and asked me to help him rocking it backwards and forwards. In a moment there was a sharp click. He jumped into the car again, pulled the starter button and away it went. 'There you are. That's your problem solved.' He said and asked me to sign the AA form to claim whatever it was the AA paid his garage. And it was yet another motoring lesson well and truly learnt. Turning to the philosophers I remembered Occam's Razor: always try the simplest explanation first and don't jump to complicated conclusions. My father always adopted this principle when dealing with engines that didn't start and it's only too true. 90% of problems with machinery are due to some silly little faults, such as a loose wire or a drop of water in the wrong place, and can be put right if you know what it is. And that was the *raison d'etre* of the Automobile Association. Perhaps it's true of the whole of life?

So my motoring experience continued and I learned about dynamos – three brush ones – when they stopped charging, and about wheel bearings when they were insufficiently greased. One of the tapered bearings on the front wheel of the Ford started to get very noisy and I had to have it stripped down and a new bearing fitted. Labour and parts amounted to the whole of three shillings and sixpence – a minor lesson but still a lesson.

Later that year the Army decided to move me to Retford and stationed me with the Second Regiment of the Royal Horse Artillery, where the main education centre for which I was responsible, was based. It was all that such a regiment might be expected to be, except that the guns were no longer pulled by horses. Nevertheless it was slightly eccentric, for example, the

Adjutant had his own horse which lived with the regiment and occasionally he would bring it into the Officers' Mess in the middle of dinner. The Colonel was reputed to have been a magnificent field officer and led a Brigade in the campaign in Italy during the Second World War. Soldiers told me that men would follow him anywhere and that he was always in the midst of the dangers he led his men into. In peacetime he took the Army with a pinch of salt and found himself demoted to Colonel. So far as I could see this didn't worry him a scrap. He was simply not interested in putting any unnecessary pressure on himself or the officers and men of his regiment. He was in the habit of disappearing on Thursdays and reappearing on Tuesdays. In fact I recall having to see him one Tuesday afternoon and he rushed in apologising and saying how difficult it was to fit everything into the week.

The camp was a pleasant place to be in. I was particularly friendly with the Medical Officer, a young Scottish doctor, with whom I shared a variety of rather intellectual interests, and I had an excellent and humorous RAEC (Royal had been added to the AEC) Sergeant-Major to run the centre, who was later at university with me. The messing charges were high and the food wasn't too wonderful. In fact it was twice what it cost at the REME units and there was one just a few miles away at Tuxford. The Sergeant in charge of the kitchen had been a chef at the Savoy and it didn't go unnoticed that every time I stayed to lunch there there was quite a spectacular menu. Those REME officers knew how to look after themselves. Not only were they good at making themselves comfortable but they always had people who were good with cars, which was not surprising. The idea of making another move floated through my head rather frequently. In the other direction, just up the road, was the Sixth Royal Tank Regiment – all these regiments had distinguished themselves during the war – which also had a rather eccentric Adjutant. He was a large rather jovial man and had a 1927 Austin Chummy from which almost everything was missing. He kept it on a small grass hillock just outside the regimental office and when he wanted to go out in it, he pushed it down the hill and jumped in as soon as the engine fired. As far as I remember the hood was missing. He had a piece of canvas he threw over it when it was raining. The dynamo was missing and the starter motor didn't work and it certainly didn't have a car battery. It ran on the magneto and as far as I remember he had a small motorbike battery, which he charged in the workshops and connected directly to the lights in the winter. In spite of all this I can never recall an occasion when he failed to get away. If he didn't need something he saw no reason to bother about it. It was men like that that made the British Army what it was in wartime, especially when its back was against the wall, or rather the sea, as it was at Dunkirk.

My next move was to Tuxford, which hadn't been too hard to arrange. At one of our monthly meetings at District HQ in Nottingham I had a word with my Colonel and it was duly settled. The Army has a wonderful bureaucracy. If you know how to fiddle it, it's surprisingly easy to get things done and cut through the red tape. An example occurred soon after I had settled down at Tuxford. In those immediate post-war years wood, like almost everything else, not excluding cars and food, was extremely scarce. The technical colleges at that time needed it very badly for their carpentry courses and I had learned that there was a Command Return Supply Depot at Sleeford in Lincolnshire, where there was a large stock of it, returned as surplus from army units from all over Northern Command. It was merely a matter of putting two and two together. I'd requisition a 3 ton truck and go with one of my Sergeants to Sleeford and fill it with wood, then we'd go round the technical colleges in my area. The Sergeants and the Sergeant-Major at my centre at Retford loved it. It was great fun for them and if we got found out I would be the one to 'carry the can'. The result was amazing. I arranged courses and lectures all over the place. No one could understand how I did it. Fortunately the heads of the colleges

kept their mouths shut and even the General was delighted as he
was, as I've already said, particularly keen on preparing National
Servicemen for 'civvy street' when their time was up. There was
a feeling that you were somehow wasting your time in the army
now that the war was over and doing that sort of thing literally
transformed the attitude of those young soldiers. I remember on
one occasion discovering that one of the young soldiers at
Retford was going to start a fish and chip shop with his brother
when he was demobbed so I went to the local fish and chip shop
in the town and asked if they would like the help of a soldier on
two or three evenings a week. He learnt a lot about the trade in
those few months before he was demobilised.

You could hardly imagine a more friendly unit than the outfit
at Tuxford. From the Commanding Officer, a young Major,
down they made the army formalities seem little more than a
pretence and I got everybody's support for what I was doing.
Captain Bloxham, the Adjutant, had an almost new Series E
Morris 8, of which I was extremely envious. David Higgs, the
son of Higgs of Higgs Motors in Birmingham, the largest
electric motor manufacturing firm in the country, arrived as a
Second Lieutenant in REME. He had one of his firm's Austin 8's
and I was even more envious of that and enjoyed it enormously
whenever we went out for a spin in it. I remember him telling
me that the firm, which had quite a large number of them,
found that it paid them only to have third party insurance on
the whole fleet, based on their calculations of the cost of the
accidents over a longish period. I nearly bought an older one
(1939) in London, but after having an AA check decided not to.
I gave my Y Model a few knocks over the year, not so much
owing to reckless driving, but on account of the awful rod
brakes which constantly went out of adjustment. Once they
failed just as a lorry with its tailboard down pulled up right in
front of me and the tailboard crunched gently into my radiator
grill. I don't think the driver even noticed it, although it made a
prominent impression on my car, but seemed to have no effect

on the sweet running of my somewhat unfortunate machine. The amount of respect that other drivers exhibited on account of it was quite remarkable. I remember being vividly impressed as I was coming down the hill towards the Mill Hill roundabout on weekend leave. It is necessary to know that no definite system of priority on the approach to roundabouts had been developed then. It was thought that the main road had priority but it was often difficult to tell which was the major road. It is also necessary to know that London taxis at that time always thought that they automatically had priority and that the whole of London ought to be ready to come to a halt for them. Anyway the point of my story is that as I was approaching the roundabout a taxi driver coming in my direction must have seen me and slammed his brakes on. In the light of the prevailing customs it was an experience never to be forgotten.

My envy was not altogether unreasonable. I really did need a better car for the amount of travelling I was doing. So one weekend, when I was at home on leave, I dropped into Jack Surtees' shop and he said he knew where I could get a Series E, a brand new Morris Eight Series E for £500. Staggering as such a sum was, this really did seem to be an opportunity not to be missed. I'd borrow something from the bank, something from my mother and hope to get a few pounds for my by now rather battered Ford 8. I went with my mother to see it. My father was away. She also thought it was smashing. It was so new and shining. I paid for it. I drove it home and got cold feet. I had gone beyond, far beyond, the bounds of financial prudence. So what was I to do? I drove it straight back to the showroom and saw the salesman who sold it to me. He gave me my cheque back immediately. Salesmen were not like salesmen today. They didn't need to have the skill of the spider. They had a hundred other flies ready and willing to fly into their web. I often wondered since if I had made a big mistake.

Talking about slick salesmen reminds me of one of the things we used to do when I was at home on a Saturday evening. We went round to see Captain Console. He was a war correspondent on the Daily Express in the First World War and lost a leg and ended up with a job in the War Office. He was still there and he was the man to go to if you wanted anything fixed up in that quarter. His stories about his days as a young journalist were sources of endless amusement. The exploits of a young Irishman called Magee never failed to astound and delight. Magee always managed to get the best stories and then race round all the phone boxes in the vicinity and cut the lines to the enragement of all the others hoping to get their stories in first. The highlight perhaps was his description of a visit to a rehearsal of one of Oscar Wilde's plays directed by Wilde himself. The reason we knew the family was because when my mother took me to school in Forest Hill, when I was six, Adrian Console, who was also six and was with his mother, created such an almighty rumpus that she had to take him home. However he did turn up on the occasional day and began to settle down. I don't think he ever got into any great trouble, but he was always doing really interesting things at home. I liked him and would often go with him to see what he was up to. I saw him once when I was still in the Army and I remember taking him for a drive in my car. I learnt then that he was in the second-hand car business and he showed me a rather large wrist watch he had with the works removed and some pieces of metal inside, and demonstrated how he could tap on various part of the car and make a rattling sound. The poor prospective vendor had had his confidence in his car shaken by the time he returned from a demonstration drive and the moment for clinching a deal arrived. I doubt if he ever did half the clever things he talked about but, like his father, loved a good story. The last I heard of him was in a letter from Hollywood where he seemed to be doing interesting and exciting work. I'm sure he would have been brilliant at special effects.

On the third attempt I did succeed in getting a better car but my luck that third time was certainly questionable. It was a black

1939 Ford Prefect – incidentally the Y model was blue, in spite of being a Ford – with a crocodile type bonnet and it cost the more manageable sum of £250. Again I went to the AA but this time in the area where I was stationed. I went to the garage that was selling it at the prearranged time only to find that the inspector was well settled in with the proprietor, and he informed me that he had already examined the car. He gave it an absolutely A1 report and it certainly appeared to be in excellent condition. Subsequently it turned out that it had a substantial list of faults, the steering and brakes among them. Fortunately the garage accepted responsibility and carried out the repairs at no further cost to me. The engine was noisy and burning oil and by chance some months later I met a mechanic who lived near my grandfather's house and worked at Dagenham Motors just off Oxford Street. By then most things had been put right, and having had a good look at the car, pronounced it to be in pretty good condition but that it would be worth fitting a recondi-tioned engine. He said that he would fit it himself and that it would cost me twenty pounds. In those days any repair that cost more than three shillings and sixpence was reckoned to be a financial disaster. However he did it and it really did make rather a good car of it – the proof of the pudding was in the driving during the rest of my time in the Army. In addition I learnt a lesson or two from my kind mechanic. After the engine had been run in he took me for a drive in the car in Central London. Hyde Park Corner had no traffic lights in those days. 'I'll show you how to deal with this,' he said, as we approached it and went straight into the traffic merging from all sides, with breath-taking decisiveness. Everything seemed to fit in with his approach without any discomfort or road rage and we emerged safely and almost effortlessly on the other side. I felt that the other drivers almost wanted to say thank you to him for being so clear. After that when I returned north I went straight to the Ford agents in Worksop and bought a book of service vouchers – five minor and one major – for twenty-one shillings, and I had

very good service from the Prefect and a very good allowance
from the army to soften the effect of my original outlay.

Chapter 3

The Real World

After my time in the Army a new phase in my life began. I had to face the rigours of civilian life. I liked the idea of living in a university town which had a life of its own and Oxford seemed to fit the picture I had in mind – another escape perhaps? Dick Thomas was living in Oxford at the time when I was demobbed and as far as I remember was reading mathematics at one of the colleges. He had rented a house just off the Ifley Road where he and his wife set up home, albeit in the most unconventional of senses for those days. I went to stay with them for a couple of weeks and decided to advertise my Ford Prefect in the Oxford Mail. I could no longer afford to run a car of such grand style in the academic world I was just approaching. My ad brought many replies and I sold it with little difficulty for £300. Its new owner gave me the money in one pound notes in a brown paper bag. I had never before experienced so much money in my hands. I tied it up tightly and, for some unaccountable reason, kicked it round the garden. Some primitive sense of jubilation and power must have explained it. Remember a thousand pounds or so could buy you a good house in London and my bag of notes a cottage in the country in those post- war days. To return to cars Dick had a 10 hp Hillman Minx saloon of the early thirties and thereafter for the rest of my stay I had to rely on being a passenger in the Hillman, and now I would have to look for some sort of car for myself at that lowly level. My father had a 1931 Austin 7 lying around somewhere, which he had used during the war. He never got rid of any machinery he had acquired and I could certainly use that. It had the standard saloon body, the short wheelbase and the rear wheel arches that cut into the doors. It rattled like the devil and nothing seemed to fit, but in spite of that it ran quite well. I think my father was pleased to see it on the road again. My first task, however, was to find a place at one of the colleges, which was not easy when so many men were returning from the services. The procedure then was to apply to individual colleges and hope. No systematic procedure existed such as there is today. After a couple of failures I had a positive response from St. Peter's Hall (now College). I was sent the college exam papers to do at home and the Master, Canon Howard, suggested that we might meet on Paddington Station and have the interview in London. I wrote to say that I was intending to spend a week in Oxford with friends and if it would be more convenient for him I could come to the college, and that is precisely what happened. All this may seem far removed from motorcars, but in fact the attitude of the college and university authorities was to play a big part in my automotive career.

At about this time a chap who had just sold his garage business bought my parents' house, but we rented a flat in it until we found another suitable house. He was a lively character who was keen on motor racing and regretted that he had not taken it up as a career and who was also a rather a good mechanic with a slick but systematic approach to engineering. All his old customers came round to him with their troubles believing Bill'll fix it. From my point of view he arrived at just the right time. The army had spoilt me. I had got used to always having a car at my beck and call. The Austin Seven was all right but I craved the luxury of a Y Model. The Prefect I had eradicated from my dreams when I sold it. The term started and I wasn't officially allowed to keep a car in Oxford. I had to work rather hard because after two terms you had the Prelims exam and they chucked you out rather ruthlessly if you did not succeed. I kept the Austin with friends on the outskirts of town and used it at weekends. It had the petrol tank just behind the dashboard and just above the engine.

The seams had cracked and petrol was seeping out rather dangerously. My friends told me of a man with a garage a few miles north of Oxford. He'd sort me out they said. He had been an engineer with the tank corps in North Africa during the war. So I drove up there one bright Saturday morning. He hadn't much time but said 'Yes I'll do it.' 'Shall I empty the tank?' I asked as he approached with his welding gear. 'No,' he said, 'petrol doesn't burn.' I thought he'd have to empty the tank and blow it out with the airline. He explained to me afterwards that he was an engineer with the tanks before Alamein and you didn't have time to fiddle about when Rommel was just up the road. I kept well back while he was doing it but it was beautifully done and ended my troubles in that direction. Winter came and the vacation and I went back to London. Some friends from Wales came to stay with us just after Christmas. They had just bought a new Morris Minor at the time of the Motor Show and they let me drive it. It left an indelible impression. What a contrast it was with the shaking and rattling of an Austin 7 that really was on it last wheels, although that's a bit unfair because the wheels really were quite good. It was the rest of the car that didn't seem to be. I had arranged to go down to visit a friend in the farthest depths of Dorset in the new year. That week it started to snow with a vengeance, and most of Southern England was snow and ice bound. It got worse and worse. Should I set out, especially should I set out in that Austin 7? That was the question. I did. It was a bit like the North Pole, except that I felt there was probably tarmac under the white surface. I drove at a snail's pace for mile upon mile. I hardly dared touch the brake or jerk the steering wheel as I went through London and then on through Salisbury

and on to the Dorset border. Only then did the grip of the great
freeze up seem to relax a little and as I went south, roads which
I could recognise as roads, began to appear. The Austin behaved
valiantly and it was a proof that all that doesn't glitter may just
possibly be gold. I grew to like it and even more to develop a
fundamental confidence in the species that helped to prepare
me for the adventures that lay ahead. I went for a few drives
round Dorset and back to London, which the car took rattling-
ly and shakingly in its stride. Later that year, I think it might
have been Easter time, when I was back in London from Oxford
a major motoring event occurred. Somewhere or another I came
across a 1929 Austin 7 with a coach built body. It had two front
seats – fine for a couple of adults – and a seat about six inches in
depth in the back, which could accommodate a couple of small
children or one small adult perched sideways on it. It was for
sale for something like £75. I asked for a drive in it and had
hardly gone a hundred yards before I knew that I wanted it. It
held together. It was all of a piece. There were bumps, of course,
but they were bumps that the whole car joined in. The long and
the short of it was that I asked Bill to come along and have a look
at it and settled on it without more ado. We were still renting the
flat from Bill and we were to do so for a couple more years. I
knew that my mother had her eye on the doctor's house across
the road. It had a splendid conservatory, a fine garden and, from
my point of view most important of all, a coach house at the
bottom of the garden, which will crop up later in the story. Dr.
MacKay was getting on and one day he would retire and go back
to Scotland to enjoy his twilight years. We knew the MacKays
well and were frequent visitors to their house.

The Austin Seven was fine except for the engine. Bill had
warned me about it when he first went to check it. The big-ends
were slightly noisy, the main bearings had the characteristic
rumble of Austin Sevens and it was prone to burn more oil than
I was happy about. Bill said it would be best to take the engine
out and rebuild it: new pistons, new valves, new main bearings,

reground crankshaft, white metalled big-ends, in other words, the lot. And he did it for the amount I had managed to get knocked off the original price, which had the added advantage that I was able to watch it closely and act as an engineer's mate. It was great experience in preparation for what I was later to do myself.

The car ran beautifully, but as was the case in those times, it had to be carefully run in at less than 30 mph for 500 miles. You put a notice in the rear window, 'RUNNING IN', which you often saw around then, but which I haven't seen for years, I suppose, with more accurate modern machining. I drove it with the utmost care for the first hundred miles or so. Then a devastating blow was to befall. Dick Thomas had given up his flat in Oxford and found an unused boathouse beside the Thames at Cassington off the main road to Eynsham, and made it his home. It was a mile or so down a narrow track and a single line railway cut across it about half way down. Two gates had to be opened and closed. Crossing the lines was very difficult and especially tough on an Austin Seven. As a result I left the car there on the side of the track and walked the rest of the way. I was only paying a flying visit for the evening. To my horror when I returned that night the car was not there. We were all amazed that it should have been taken from such an out-of-the-way place. I was particularly upset that it should have happened so soon after all that work had been done to it. I stayed at the boathouse and lo and behold a couple of days later the car reappeared. Someone had gone for a joy ride in it. An extra couple of hundred miles were on the clock, but no obvious damage was done although I feared that the engine might have been abused. Still I was glad to get it back looking reasonably safe and sound. Only time would tell. Dick had bought one of the old army landing craft which were also used for constructing Bailey bridges and was building a superstructure on it to convert it into his home, which over the course of time he managed to do very successfully. The barges were going cheap so I thought I'd do the same. Why not? I built the superstructure but never found the time to achieve the same degree of sophistication that Dick had achieved, I believe, at the cost of his university career. One day Dick came in to see me with a rather urgent look on his face. 'Your boat has gone,' he said, 'It broke moorings in last night's storm.' It would have gone downstream. So we set off to check at all the locks between Oxford and Cassington. We soon got news from one of the lock keepers that it was perched on a weir a little further up stream and he took us along the tow path to see it. It really was balancing half way over the weir like the coach in the film, The Italian Job. Had it gone over it would have been smashed to pieces. The kind lock keeper helped us assess the situation with his professional experience. We managed to get a rope on the back of it and slowly, slowly pulled it off the weir. The only course was to pull it ourselves along the tow path back to Cassington and then for one of us to swim across the river with the rope. How I wished I could have attached it to the Austin and towed it with the car, but there were narrow sections under a couple of bridges where I knew it would be impossible to drive the car. We had no choice but to be resigned to the possible, and the possible was what we accomplished, happy that at least the boat was undamaged.

I had to find digs as the lodgings in college were more than full, so I moved into a little hotel just over Magdalen Bridge, the Old Black Horse. It was quite comfortable and had the advantage of having a piece of waste ground across the road next to a butcher's shop. I had a builder's tarpaulin and Dick found some rustic poles including an extra long one of about 12 or 14ft and we fixed up a very serviceable lean-to garage against the butcher's wall. This was very satisfactory as undergraduates were not allowed to have cars within the city boundaries without special permission. A friend of mine, Clement Coldwells, had an Austin Chummy of about the same year as mine, but in the most appalling condition possible to imagine. The exhaust was held on with wire, the doors were about to fall off and either he or someone else had built a very evidently homemade top of, as far as I remember, hardboard. It was no wonder that he was particularly keen on mine. The doctor had retired and my mother had bought his house. In those days you couldn't leave cars out on the streets over-night without lights so the coach house and the driveway into it offered a wholly new potential for collecting cars. A black Y Model in very good condition came up for only £100. It was irresistible. I decided I would offer Clement a part exchange: his car plus £50 for mine with just one stipulation that if he ever decided to sell it he would give me first refusal. He thought it a good deal and accepted at once, especially as his car had stopped running altogether some weeks earlier. I asked Bill to come over with me in his car to assess the situation. He took one look and said, 'We won't bother trying to start it,' and took a tow rope out and hitched it on to the front axle beam. I prepared myself for the hair raising ride that I knew was about to follow. We went over cobblestones and the old tram lines, bouncing from side to side, down the Old Kent Road and finally back to Forest Hill. There was only one good thing about that car: it was absolutely ideal for me to practise my new skills as a mechanic without worrying that I might harm it. I got the engine going without too much help, I tightened the door hinges and I fixed the exhaust pipe with some clips and some gun gum. I just don't remember what I did with it in the end, but I suppose I sold it. The great thing was that I felt in a position to go ahead with the purchase of the Ford which was fine except that it jumped out of second gear as you changed up. However I learned that this was not unusual and I got quite used to holding it in. It was so good in every other way that I forgave it that small fault. Why, I even bought a radio for it and it appeared happy in its place beside the butcher when I returned to Oxford. It seemed like the height of luxury but really to fulfil my dreams I would have needed an Austin 8 like David Higgs's 1947 model, though a good 1939 model would have sufficed.

After about a year my finances again forced me to sell the

Ford. It was looking smart and I managed to convince the buyer that the little matter of slipping out of second gear was neither here nor there. I made a small profit on it and had got good service from it for a year. I was learning from my father and from Bill how to look after cars although my father was away during the week. His health was a little uncertain and the doctor suggested that he should work on a farm for a year

By now I could never be long without a motorcar of some sort and in a way the worse they were the more fun and challenging they seemed to be. By this time my friend Clement, who was a few years older than me, had begun to establish himself in his career and needed a car more in keeping with his position. He had had extremely good service out of the Austin and now happily offered it back to me for a song, which as an impoverished student I greatly appreciated. I was now in lodgings in the home of a postman a couple of miles just out of Oxford on the road out to Faringdon and Swindon. The question was whether or not I could get permission to run the car in Oxford itself and so I went to see Canon Howard, the Master of St. Peter's Hall, whom I had almost met at platform 8 on Paddington Station for my original interview. I had had bronchitis during the war and was rather susceptible to a return of it whenever I caught a cold. It would help if I could keep dry and comfortable when travelling into Oxford in the winter. The upshot of it was that the kindly Canon would agree to me having the car if I could provide him with a medical certificate indicating that it was advisable for health reasons to run it. Dr. Mackay from across the road in Forest Hill, who had seen me on a number of occasions when I was ill, was perfectly willing to provide me with the certificate and as a result I brought the little car, later to be christened by Pat Goldacre, the Mosquito, into the city of Oxford. I remember I had to fit a little green lamp on the front of the car to conform with the regulations of the Proctors, the University authorities responsible for the discipline of the students, although many were older students returning from war service and pranks were almost unheard of at that period. I lived on a prudent budget. My fees were paid for by the Government because my studies had been interrupted by National Service, and in addition I received a £5 a week grant for living expenses. Half went on my lodgings and with the other half I had to get my lunch and supper, which I only occasionally stretched to having dinner in College, finance my social life and run the car. I mostly had my lunches in one of the British Restaurants left over from the war. This cost one shilling and three pence, a fraction more than 6p in our modern artificial money, and included a drink of tea or coffee. That £300 for the Ford Prefect had given me a robust sense of independence and I no longer needed anything from my parents, except to stay with them in the vacations, but that was rather significant as I did a bit of work for Bill, which almost amounted to an apprenticeship. I often got the odd fiver for finding a car and I sometimes took him out in mine to collect a car. I remember on one occasion he asked me to take him out to collect a rather valuable car – I can't recall what it was – but it just had one fault: something was wrong with the engine timing and it sent out showers of sparks from the exhaust pipe. At night it would have been like a firework display. In the daytime the police would have been down on it with dire consequences. There were no MOTs then but the police often stopped cars they were suspicious about. Bill had bought it very cheaply and he wanted to get it home to work on the engine. He asked me to drive very closely behind him so that my car more or less concealed the horizontal firework display. This time he drove at a very modest speed and it was when I still had the black Ford 8.

Nevertheless it was nerve racking experience driving so close that I felt I could open up the windscreen and almost touch the back of his car in front. It was an unforgettable journey that seemed to go on for ever.

In Oxford I went on driving the Mosquito. One of the people I had met at the boathouse was Pat Goldacre who lived in a wonderful wooden bungalow on stilts in the middle of the woods in Shotover just outside the city in the direction of London. The bungalow had been built by an ornithologist to enable him to have a close watch on the variety of birds that inhabited the wood. I had to leave the car down on the road and follow a winding path uphill through the woods to reach it. It was unique. Pat was the librarian at St. Anthony's College and lived there with her two young children, Michael and Angela, who crop up later in my motoring story.

The car ran with surprising regularity while I was at Oxford and I had no difficulty carrying out the necessary greasing and servicing. The engine was an enormous success despite the episode with the joy rider. In fact the only trouble I can recall was an inclination on the part of the engine to boil, which was soon put right with a course of Holt's Radflush. You put the first packet in the radiator, put a blanket over it for few minutes to make it boil quickly, after which you opened the drain tap and watched all the muck come out. You then flushed it out with clean water and put a second packet of chemicals into it. It was really amazing how much better the engine ran after that little course of treatment.

None of the little troubles that occurred with my first Ford 8 seemed to plague the Mosquito. This was due partly, I suppose, to the fact that I was becoming much more experienced in driving and looking after cars, car sympathy it is sometimes called, and partly because the Austin didn't have quite the same liveliness as the Ford. The brakes were not good but that was the case with all Austin's cars and Sir Herbert Austin himself used to say, whenever anyone complained, that good brakes made bad drivers, and there is a great deal of truth in that. Nothing else makes you think and observe ahead more effectively than dodgy brakes. But the Austin 7's brakes were reliably limited and very easy to adjust. In fact the cardinal virtue of the Austin 7 is that everything is easy to get at and work on, and on the whole it lets you know in good time when anything needs attending to.

While I was at Oxford my parents moved from South London down to Norfolk where I had spent the first two and a half years of my life. We had been going down to friends for holidays most years and it had always seemed to me to be a magical place. It still does. They bought Long Row Farm at Tivetshall and let most of the fields to neighbouring farmers. Being at university I was unable to take full advantage of the wonderful farm buildings. So when the time came to leave Oxford I had decided to take the teacher's training course at London University Institute of Education, which I did in due course and found lodgings in Highbury. I remember loading the Mosquito with books and all my goods and chattels. It was the next best thing to a removal van. I never thought I would be able to cram so much into a little tiny car but I did although various things dug into my side and my head kept banging against objects behind me during the journey to London. I rented a nice little room for a pound a week. There was a piece of waste land across the road. There were many such pieces of ground in London where bombs had dropped during the war; this was useful for me then because it was, as I mentioned, illegal at that time to park cars without lights in the streets at night.

In those days it was an easy run down to the Institute in Malet Street and although there was plenty of public transport it was an awkward journey and involved several changes. The Mosquito buzzed up and down regularly. I couldn't do much with cars in those circumstances and in any case I had to concentrate on what I thought of as my other career: teaching. However an event that turned out to be highly significant from the motoring point of view did take place towards the end of my course in London, which lasted from September till the following June when I would be a fully fledged teacher. There was an old wartime airfield behind the farm and a serious proposal to open it up again for civil aircraft, which terrified my mother. In the meantime, Dr. Mackay had retired and his house was due to come up for sale. My mother saw her opportunity and bought it without hesitation. It had that coach house at the bottom of the garden that I had my eye on. It would accommodate two small cars and a fairly steep concrete driveway ran down to it with space on one side to park four or five cars and still leave room to drive up and down – just. The temptation to turn it into something like a breaker's yard was great. My mother, as far as I remember, tended to oppose this – the young even in those days could be very unreasonable – but fortunately there was adequate screening at the bottom of the garden to hide any disreputable vehicle I might be tempted to bring in, and over the next year or two I was to get away with a surprising amount. I had the Mosquito, of course, to start this new stage of my motoring adventures and Bill was just across the road to guide my work on cars and my father was often present at moments of engineering crisis.

I had heard that a fellow student from Oxford was critically ill in hospital in Cardiff and I had only a single day before some vital exam at the Institute. Nevertheless I decided to go up and see him. I set off early in the morning. So it was a journey along what now would be considered highways and byways. Anyhow I made it. I saw him and returned to London the same day, although in fact I did not actually reach London until one o'clock the following morning. It was an experience that made me realise what an Austin Seven could do, and was later to play its part in the debate in my mind about my South American trip.

A little earlier I remember my father had been rather ill and the doctor had advised him to have spell in the country so he decided he would like to try working on a farm for a year. It was one of those rare periods when he didn't have a car and I remember that he bought a very nice little Austin Seven saloon with little encouragement from me although he always had a very high regard for Austins and often talked of getting an Austin Swallow. It wasn't a Swallow but it was almost like new. I think we both became very fond of it. So we now both had Austin Sevens.

At about this time another surprise came up. In some backyard or other as I was going round I happened to see – I had learnt to keep my eyes open for cars – a rather unusual Austin Seven with a Muliner body, the top body builders for Rolls Royce. I enquired about it after managing to find the owner. 'It's no use,' he said, 'the engine's completely worn out. The big-ends have gone and the chassis's cracked across the middle.' The body was so beautiful that I was completely mesmerised by it. I wanted to have it even if I couldn't drive it. It would be a sort of museum piece in the coach house. The long and the short of it was that he said I could have it for five pounds and I had it towed home in the usual way. The body frame was made of wood and had leather stretched over it. The doors and all the fittings were delightful and I had a dream, never fulfilled, of transferring the body onto the chassis of Clement's Chummy and rebuilding the engine myself. In fact I did achieve the latter. It was the first engine I completely rebuilt myself, although with Bill's occasional supervision. The bloc was rebored and I fitted new pistons. I had big-ends remetalled and I scraped them in myself with engineer's blue. I ground in all the valves and at every stage Bill exercised the rigorous discipline he would have applied to an apprentice. My memory is that after working for about an hour on a valve he would look at it and tell me that I was beginning to get it right. Nevertheless his help was not just a one way process.

I often went out with him to fetch cars and acted as an engineer's mate, and I watched him very closely as he did various jobs and as time went by he trusted me with the simpler jobs on customers' cars. The new Austin had not creaked and groaned too badly as I sat in it being towed, and after some time and thought I considered it would be worth putting the rebuilt engine back into it. Clement's car was great for practising on. I had no fear of doing it any further harm and when I got it going I used it for a very short time and I simply cannot remember what finally happened to it. I suppose I sold it for a minute sum.

My real attention focussed on the Muliner bodied Austin
Seven. I got it going nicely and I thought if the worst came to the
worst I could bolt a couple of pieces of angle iron on to the
cracked chassis which was easy to get at because you could lift
out the wooden flooring. However the worst incident in the
whole of my motoring experience was just about to occur and
make that expedient irrelevant. The engine ran perfectly thanks
very largely to Bill's strict instructions. Flushed with that success
I started to use the car on an every day basis. I still had some
things left behind in my lodgings in Highbury so I arranged to
collect them. The main thing was a box of gramophone records,
as we called them then, the old 78s. I was going to see Bill Craig
at the London Hospital. He had been with me at Oxford and was
then completing his medical training. The journey took me to
Smithfield Market. The road used to run straight through the
centre of the market, under a great archway. Every now and
again I bent my head down to listen to the engine. I did so when
I was halfway through. I could not see that another main road
ran straight across it at right angles. There was no sign or
warning. Suddenly as I was just emerging I saw two cars about
to cut straight across in front of me to my left. In a flash I saw
that if I turned left I might avoid the cars but if I failed to there
was a pretty clear risk of a head-on collision, and if I turned
right I would almost certainly hit the first car sideways on. In a
split second I made the decision to turn right. There was an
almighty bang and the little car flew up into the air and came
down on its roof. In a moment it was transformed into a bundle
of firewood with torn pieces of leather attached to it and broken
records all over the place. The petrol tank burst and doused the
pile of wreckage in petrol. Petrol, of course, does burn in the
open air and it was a miracle that a spark didn't ignite it and a
further miracle that I crawled out from under it all unhurt apart
from a thump in the back as the car hit the road. Within minutes
a fire engine, an ambulance and two police cars arrived. They
calmed me down and the policeman questioned me. Twice he

asked 'How did it happen?' and I couldn't think of an answer. 'Well,' he said, 'did your foot slip on the throttle?' Immediately I said 'Yes' and he wrote it down saying, 'I think you've had enough trouble this evening. You don't want my report to make it worse.' Every time I thought about it I have always appreciated that little bit of kindness. The firemen cleared up the mess and turned the remains of the car back on its wheels. Bill came out with me the next day and we contrived to get it back home.

I had noticed an Austin Seven body behind a garage in Bromley on the road out to Sevenoakes. It did have a chassis but no engine, no axles and no wheels. I had the wheels, I had the axles and I had the rebuilt engine, and I was determined to see it used. It was clear that what I had would match up with what the garage had and in those days a '34 Austin Seven was much better than a '28. I'd go for it. And in fact I got it for a fiver and a bit of hard work: first putting the axles on, then towing it home and fitting the engine. It was a great success and I was happy with it – for a little time. The time to start looking for a job had arrived. I went for an interview at Long Dene School in Chiddingstone Castle in Kent. I liked John Guinness, the Headmaster. 'We like whole things here,' he said, 'we have our own farm and everybody takes part in everything.' In addition his young son had a small car frame with a motorbike engine in it. I said I would be delighted to help him running it. Furthermore there was plenty of space in the barn where he kept it to put my car(s). It all seemed pretty much to my liking but it was a boarding school and there were lots of extra duties in the evenings and as far as I remember every other weekend. I ran up and down from Chiddingstone whenever I got the chance and I did a course at the Institute of Education on a couple evenings a week. My aunt who fell off the motorbike lived at Riverhead and I could always call in there on my way just as I did before the war when she lived in my grandfather's house just outside Horniman's Gardens.

One of my favourite pupils was Ian Samwell, always known as

Sammy. Sammy Samwell was a bit of a tearaway but highly intel-
ligent and bursting with originality. He later wrote the songs for
Cliff Richards that first brought his to fame on the pop scene. At
the end of term the children often put on a show in the baronial
hall in the castle and did skits on various members of staff.
Sammy had secretly and skilfully prepared one on me in which
he acted himself and had had the help of the science teacher.
When the curtain went up there was a brilliant likeness of my
Austin Seven made of painted cardboard boxes with a seat for
Sammy inside it. He had recorded the genuine sound of my
engine running and the starter motor turning over without my
getting an inkling of what he was doing. In the scene he first
entered in an old mack, instantly recognised as mine, and
fiddled about in his pockets to find the car key in a manner that
I knew was only too plainly in character. He then got in the car
and tried the starter motor several time but the car didn't go, so
he got out and bent over the improvised starting handle and
swung it. Suddenly the engine sprung into life and he quickly
jumped back into the car to keep it going and then sat back in
the driving seat looking towards the audience with an immense
look of satisfaction beaming from his face. Then he revved up
and prepared to drive away. The recording was perfectly syn-
chronised to fit the action and then suddenly there was an
enormous bang and a flash and the curtain came down. Those
of us in the audience could have sworn that we saw the car
blown into smithereens as it was driving away. The science
teacher had supervised the rather risky device of placing a
firework behind the cardboard box on which the bonnet was
painted so that Sammy could skilfully lean over and light it
without the audience being aware. The timing was perfect and
the whole scene was executed to perfection, or almost to perfection. As I told Sammy, my car never behaved like that at the end.

Lois was one of the teachers and although it was a 'free'
school, she was older and more formidable and I'm sure there
was no playing up in her classes. On one occasion she was going

into Edenbridge to have her hair set and I offered her a lift. Although I was a teacher at that stage I think I felt more of the feelings of the pupils than I did of some of my fellow staff. I don't think we disliked Lois but we did feel she was formidable and it provoked something in me. I fear I gave her a rather hairy ride into town. When I offered to wait and drive her back, I got a polite, 'No.' Her appointment would take some time and she didn't want to delay me. She must have gained the impression that I was in rather a hurry. Thereafter I detected many references to that journey from both staff and pupils and my standing in the eyes of the latter was distinctly elevated.

A few other motoring highlights occurred during that year at Long Dene. One concerned a customer/friend of Bill's, who had a 1934 Austin Cambridge 10hp saloon in the pink of condition. A teacher at school, who had come over from Australia, wanted a very good car to go on an extended tour of the Continent during the coming summer. I knew that the Austin was going to be for sale as its owner, who was always rude about my cars, was getting a much later model. He called mine 'mobile dustbins'. He would always greet me with, 'Hello John, how are your mobile dustbins getting on?' It was hard to mind because he always said it in such a good-natured way. Nevertheless the Cambridge was always in spic and span condition, and I loved driving it. It was arranged for me to take it down to Chiddingstone for inspection. 'Don't put too much rubbish in it,' was his final remark. He needn't have worried because it never came back. Its new Owner fell in love with it as soon as he set eyes on it and I didn't blame him. I heard later that he was having a wonderful holiday travelling for thousands of miles round Europe in the beautiful Austin. I couldn't deny being a little envious of him. By this time I has advanced on to another Ford. This time it was maroon with what was then called a shooting brake body. In fact it was a van with windows and a few bits of wood stuck on it. The significant fact however was that it had a lower ratio back axle so that it had more pulling power but less speed. It had a slight whine in the axle but it was good. The appropriate additives dealt with that for all the time I had it. You could load lots in it and there was room to sleep in it very comfortably. In fact you could say it was the forerunner of the camper van and camp in it I did. That Summer I went up to the Lake District in it. I thought I would just potter around and meet people as I went. However by chance, not design, I happened to bump into Ingrid, the assistant matron at the school, who was staying in the Lake District for her holiday and we had some happy walks and drives together. The Ford behaved well except for a few leaks on rainy days, mainly on Ingrid. It coped with the steep and winding hills mainly because by now I had learned to cope with the Ford's rod brakes very much better than I did when I first started to drive, and I could give them frequent enough adjustment to be more or less safe.

The year was moving fast even before the Summer holidays and the school was making an indelible impression on me but its future appeared bleak, mainly for economic reasons. I had completed the first part of the course at the Institute of Education. At the end of the Summer I decided to go on to do a research degree. My parents were going to move to Bromley so that meant the end of the coach house, a very sad prospect indeed. It was necessary to dispose of several of the cars I'd acquired at insignificant cost. The first was a Triumph 7 with a shooting brake body and the hand brake on the prop shaft that was almost unusable when you were moving. The car shook from end to end and I'm sure would have fallen apart completely after a few serious attempts to bring it to a halt on the road. It gave a special meaning to the idea of an emergency stop. The second was another Y Model shooting brake in very poor condition. I was not really sorry to see those two go but the third was a lovely little 1929 Chummy: red, smart and exciting with only one little fault I was sure I could put right quite easily, probably due to a damaged leather coupling on the propshaft. Its hood was like new and the side screens were perfect. I couldn't bear to see it go. It had cost me only twelve pounds and ten shillings but I felt its value couldn't be measured in terms of money. I took it down to a piece of waste ground at the bottom of the road and put a cover on it and tied it up securely, until, as I thought, I could find somewhere to keep it safely. However when I went back a few weeks later it had been severely vandalised, and I simply had to give up on it. This left the red Ford and the central character in my motoring career, the 1925 Austin Chummy. I sold the Ford and kept the Chummy as my regular transport. This reminds me of one amusing and memorable incident. It was at the time when Khruschev and Bulganin were visiting London. I had moved into the university lodgings but had come home at the weekend. As I was returning I approached Westminster Bridge, suddenly I was caught up in the motorcade, and police on motorbikes flew at me from every direction, waving their arms desperately to get out of the way. I could see the two of them in the car in front looking round, I suppose, to see what all the fuss was about. I've often wondered who was more surprised, them or me? It was hard to know where to go with motorbikes flying at me from every direction, but I did eventually extricate myself by slowing down almost to a halt so that they could get away.

I used the Ford for a while during the first university term. I was given a study to myself in the university library but as no further grant was available, I was again up against the finance question rather acutely. To solve this I did a couple of days tutoring at Carlisle and Gregsons. The institution had quite a distinguished past. Numerous well known people had been there to be coached for their examinations. One was the son of a US Airforce General. At that time a number of children of US military personnel were there. Moving from pillar to post their education had suffered and they then had to be prepared for GCE. That was fine, but the Principal was certainly unusual with rather mystical ideas and held a high position in the Druids' organisation, and I went with him to a few things out of curiosity. As we drove along he would say every now and again, 'a witch lives in that house'. I remember I took him down to West Wycombe to see what the Hell Fire Club had been up to in the 18th century. Coming home we were going down a very steep hill when the Ford's brakes failed completely. I didn't say it, but I remember thinking: 'I could use a bit of your magic now.' I just managed to turn the car towards the hedge and crash it into an area of soft foliage before anything worse happened. I crawled home with my visibly shaken passenger beside me and I don't think he ever asked me to take him out again. Nonetheless his institution's money was very useful and for the first year in combination with living at home I scraped along quite comfortably.

Another very important person in my life with motor cars at this particular juncture was Jimmy Childs, the youngest son of my mother's best friend Alice Childs. Jimmy had one of the early Morris Minors of about 1931 and he had reached the point when he'd done just about everything that could be done to it. He also, I believe, had a slight guilt complex towards me. When I was 9 and he was, I think, 12 or 13, I went with my mother to visit Mrs Childs. Mr Childs was killed in the First World War. Jimmy was in and we went into the garden and lit a bonfire. I always knew that exciting things were bound to happen when visiting Jimmy Childs: a real model steam engine with methylated spirit burning underneath it, or some piece of amazing machinery, or even on one occasion a cage full of carrier pigeons. On this occasion it was the bonfire. As I say Jimmy always explained impressive things. This time it was how you could move your hands rapidly through flames without getting burnt and he demonstrated it with a candle running his finger through the flame. This was something utterly new and amazing to me. In his enthusiasm he said he could swing me round right through the flames of the bonfire and I wouldn't feel a thing. I was a bit reluctant about this but I didn't want to seem too sissy. I had short trousers on and I felt the flames just tingling my legs, so he went on several times round and I suppose became slightly giddy and began to topple over sideways landing my legs right in the middle of the fire. He pulled me out like lightening, terrified of the awful thing he had done. My legs didn't tingle then and I was in pain for weeks if not months. I never mentioned it to him in later years. It was not one of those things we could laugh at afterwards. But it did have one benefit: whenever Christian martyrs being burnt at the stake were mentioned in scripture lessons I felt secretly that I had a superior understanding of the situation to the rest of the class.

Bill was away a good deal at this time and Jimmy would come over if I asked him and he was free, and give invaluable help with a great variety of jobs on my cars. We would visit breakers' yards together and search for parts. It's marvellous to share your jubilation with a fellow enthusiast when you discover some rare part – far better than winning the lottery. Poor Jimmy had adenoids and had to go into hospital quite often and later died during an operation in his early thirties. At this time, however, the Morris Minor presented no further challenges and he sold it for a very good price and bought a Y-Model Ford which he proceeded to treat in exactly the same way, even giving it an impeccable respray. To go out in it was to experience exactly what it must have been like in 1937 when it first hit the highway.

My university life was drawing to a final close in 1956. I had had to complete a final thesis and when that was over I felt I would want and need a decent break and yet there wasn't time to organise anything on the scale I would have liked. So when a friend and fellow student told me that he had planned to go on a camping holiday in the south of France, I was really interested. He was going with his fiancée and she had insisted on having another woman friend coming to chaperon them and asked if I would like to join them as there was a spare seat in her new Austin A30. It was a disaster. The girls wanted to stop all day at the fashionable shops in Paris and in Lyon and in every other town on the way down. My friend and I thought we would never reach the Mediterranean. We did in the end get to Frejus and found a camp site and after a day or two left the girls there while we went on into Italy. We had a pleasant few days there before coming back to pick the girls up for the return journey with memories of delicious Italian food and wine, but not having seen the most interesting sights in that fascinating country. The engagement was broken off. My friend said the holiday had been very worthwhile for him but he feared that I had had a rather raw deal. I was glad for him and I must say engagements in which both parties get a chance to know more about each other before getting inextricably involved may not be such a bad idea.

My friend Barbara May who was at the Institute of Education with me – and how I wished she had been on that holiday with me instead – went to teach in Leeds and I went down to Alresford Place in Hampshire, an unusual special school, but that is the subject of another book. The following year I did a tour of Northern Europe in the 1934 Morris Series 1 tourer, which I bought from a car salesman right out in the depths of Hampshire, and had a wonderful holiday with Barbara. The car behaved perfectly through Belgium, Holland, Germany and Denmark and I almost forgave it for being a Morris and not an Austin. I thought it gave us a luxurious ride and of course it had hydraulic brakes – one up on the old Y-Model. During my first year at Alresford Place School I had used my famous Chummy but that story fits into a later chapter. The following year we made another great European trip down through France to the Cote d'Azure and round the islands by boat and the back through Switzerland and again through France. Again in the wonderful little Morris tourer but this time not without trouble. I had gone to a great deal of effort preparing the car. I had taken the wheels off and the brake drums and checked all the brakes and put a dash of grease in appropriate places, checked the linings, serviced everything thoroughly. I even stripped the dynamo right down, put in new brushes, cleaned the commutator and washed the whole thing very carefully in petrol. I really was determined to have everything as near perfect as possible.

Humber 8

At home outside Flordon Hall in Norfolk with
the first car I knew but don't remember.

Herbert Austin tries out his first four cylinder car with a puff of smoke in 1905.

Assembling the first 8 hp Rover in 1908 – how cars ought to be constructed.

The Rover 8 engine, air cooled, horizontally opposed.

Early magneto assembly line at Highland Park, Detroit.

The 250,000 Model-T made in Britain in David Copperfield setting.

One of my aunts on her motorbike in the 1920's.

The 'Old Crocks Race' as we called it in 1931, the London to Brighton Run.

The first time I went into a real aeroplane on a visit to Croydon Aerodrome in about 1933.

The 11 hp AC, the first car I remember.

The rugged 10 hp Swift on the top of the Honister Pass on a cloudy vintage afternoon. The saloon version followed the AC when I got rather too big to squeeze in the middle of the front seat.

The Singer 8 Junior identical to the first car I owned which ran like a sewing machine when it was not in trouble.

The identical Ford to the 1935 Y-Model I learnt to drive on.

The rather superior 1939 Ford Prefect which followed the Y-Model – the actual car!

7 hp Triumph Super Seven - a real Vintage photograph.

Jimmy Childs with with his 1931 Morris Minor at Long Row Farm in Norfolk.

One of the Austin 7 saloons my father had just after the War, which I took over afterwards.

The Chummy with the new Mini in Managua.

The launch of *Coleman's Drive* at Smiths in Southampton.

Tony Hutchin's 1923 works racer 696cc engine.

Incentives to leave the car at home

From the Editor of New European

Sir, I loved Simon Jenkins's article, "Tear up these roads to ruin" (May 31). The message is almost 40 years overdue but it is good to hear it spelt out loud and clear at last.

I believe there was some question in Brussels a few years ago about putting out a directive barring all cars over 20 years old from being driven on public roads. I tried to say then that, if Brussels wanted to do something really good for a change, it would ban all cars *under* 20 years old.

Some sort of compromise has to be found, and I believe that encouraging people to think of their car as a mode of peripheral transport could help greatly: public transport must be for normal use, and the car perceived as a special treat for special occasions.

Why not give a railcard with every annual car tax disc for the motorist and his family to ride on buses and trains at, say, half fare? That, combined with allowing the price of fuel to go through the roof (through taxation if necessary), should provide a pretty effective incentive for most of us to relax and let somebody else ferry us about.

Yours faithfully,
JOHN COLEMAN,
Editor, *New European*,
14-16 Carroun Road, SW8.
June 2.

My letter to *The Times*.

30/3/92
SOLD TO MR COLEMAN
AUSTIN ALLEGRO
FOR £135.00
CASH Reg No
VPJ 809M of
A. HOLME'S

27 THORTON AVE
STREATHAM SW16
8TG

Receipt for the Allegro, still in regular use!

The Chummy at the Daily Telegraph Travel and Adventure Show at Olympia.

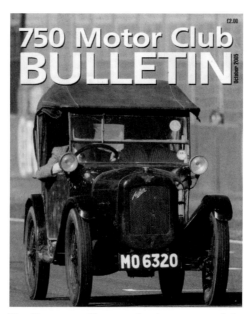

The Chummy at Silverstone for the centenary of the Austin Motor Company after three laps round the circuit.

We stayed for a couple of weeks near Nice where we had met an interesting Danish couple with a fantastic new Volvo which I was rather envious of whenever we went out in it, which was quite often since they couldn't go out in the Morris as I'd taken the back seats out for our camping gear and fitted a special top which I could lock. I was rather proud of it. It had legs underneath on hinges so it could be used as a camping table as well as a secure cover for our equipment What happened next I was not so proud of. As we were leaving Nice the dynamo stopped charging. I fiddled about with it but could find nothing wrong. As it was of the three-brush type I knew it was not safe to go on without the risk of burning it out. The battery was well charged up and I knew that in the daytime it would run on a negligible amount of current. There was a Lucas agents at Avignon and if the worst came to the worst I could get the battery charged on the way. We arrived there at around lunchtime but just in time to get their electrician to put the dynamo on the tester. He had a bottle of wine on the bench beside him. He seemed to get good readings and yet the wretched thing wasn't charging. Every time he tested it and didn't get the reading he wanted he would exclaim 'This dynamo makes me thirsty,' and have another swig from his bottle of wine. In the end he found one tiny strand of wire from the brushes touching on the metal at the side. It must have got very slightly caught up as I put the casing back. Hell, I thought, I'd probably have had none of this trouble if I'd not tried to be so darned careful and left the dynamo alone in the first place.

From there we went on up into Switzerland and stayed for a couple of weeks camping on the edge of Lake Geneva in a beautiful log cabin with straw mattresses. How different it was from a couple of years earlier. We did go into the city, but Barbara had no more desire to stay than I did. The next lap of the route was pretty directly across France. I somehow got involved in a race with a 2 CV. I beat him on the hills and he shot ahead on the downhill stretches. This went on for several hundred miles but we never stopped to exchange impressions, I suspect that it is something that neither of us will ever forget when the motoring experiences of our lives come to mind.

The only trouble with the Morris was in the winter. One bitter Sunday night in January I drove back from London. The sidescreens were in poor condition and didn't fit very well. I grew colder and colder until I could hardly bear it any longer. My mind was made up and I went back to the chap in Ropley from whom I'd bought it. 'Have you got a saloon of some sort?' I asked. 'Nothing you're likely to want,' he replied. 'Well, have you got anything I'm not likely to want?' I ventured to ask further. A 1939 badly resprayed Hillman Minx was his answer. I hated it but in fact it served me very well through the rest of that winter while I was searching for what I really wanted. I remembered that Morris Minor our friends had in 1948. I wanted one of those but the model with fixed side windows, not sidescreens. I'd had quite enough of those freezing nights with the Morris. By an amazing stroke of luck someone in the village had exactly the car I wanted at the best price I could possibly expect: a black Morris Tourer with 918cc side valve engine and a fawn vynal hood which fitted snugly against the side window frames. How could I wish for more? And only 18 months old. Why it was as good as new! A heater was not fitted as standard but well muffled up I could now survive any weather. I sometimes felt I could drive to the North Pole in it. As spring and summer came on I had a short spell of wonderful driving before I willingly parted with it to lay the financial foundation for my journey through the Americas.

Chapter 4

The Terrible Mistake

Thomas de Quincey wrote about travelling in the 18th century. He argued that moving at more than thirteen miles per hour was a waste of time, or rather of experience. You couldn't appreciate existence around you and therefore you were in a kind of time vacuum. But even that restraint would not have been enough to make the Red Flag Act superfluous. Another Act of Parliament set the speed limit at 20mph and according to Stenson Cooke the police had a fine old time of it setting traps to catch motorists doing 21mph on the clear open roads. The story of how the AA changed all that is graphically told in his book with the subtitle, 'A Romantic History of the AA'. Time wore on and the idea of motoring for the millions was put forward by Henry Ford when he set up the world's first assembly lines and the notion of mass production was born. It was certainly a seductive idea and pregnant with political potential in the modern democratic world which was developing in tandem with the mechanical results of the Industrial Revolution. Herbert Austin, great man as he was, also helped to give reality to the concept with his amazing little Austin Seven. But the man above all who saw the political potential in the idea was Adolf Hitler. The promise of a Volkswagen, a people's wagon, for every German family had an immense lure for galvanising the

German nation behind his war plans. The autobahns added, no doubt, to the appeal of the VW although I suspect the real motive for them was a military one.

Neither Ford nor Austin liked the idea of the 'throw away' car that was developing. Even before the Second World War the idea of buying a new car every two years was being floated around. Herbert Austin countered this in his adverts in which he told the public: 'You buy a car but you invest in an Austin.' Contrary to the instincts of the original Henry Ford the firm had gone in for making cheap 'Tin Lizzies', and the popular joke was if you can't afford a car, buy a Ford.

The war came in 1939 and put the car more than in its place; on blocks in locked up garages, but even that had some advantages. The roads were mainly clear and safe and perfect for the bicycle. I remember going for some wonderful rides in the countryside in Kent when we lived at Shadoxhurst near Ashford, and then later around Windsor. Except for the war it was a wonderful time. The bicycle really was the king of the road although farmers got a little petrol for their vans and tractors. I had been very ill with scarlet fever and bronchitis in the early days of the war and so I spent much time at home. We had a bungalow with seven acres of woodland behind it with a lawn, a substantial clearing with a pond on the edge of the woods and several sheds for chickens. I felt I was in wonderland. I kept chickens and ducks and geese and went to a little private school at the end of the lane which was evacuated from London. One day I went into Ashford market by bus. I was twelve at the time. I took all the money I had earned from eggs and chickens I had sold, which amounted to a fortune of four or five pounds. I didn't see any birds I wanted but I did see a man selling baby rabbits at only 3 pence each and it crossed my mind that I could branch out into a new line of husbandry. I had an empty chicken house in the garden which would just suit them. So I asked the man how much he would charge me to deliver them in his van. 'A shilling,' he said and I could get a lift in his van and that would save me three pence or four pence on my bus fare home. The deal was done. I had a substantial rabbit business, a hundred and fifty to be precise! I don't remember the make of the van. I was more interested in the colour of the rabbits and just a little worried about what my mother would say. I think she was rather too surprised to object at the time but little by little the majority of them disappeared at night until I was left with only a reasonable number.

I had had a brand new Silver Fox bicycle just before the war and it was giving me wonderful service. Maybe all this stuff about bikes and rabbits has not really got much to do with motor cars but in a way it has. Ten or so years ago I used to join a friend in the Veteran Cycle club on the rides around the countryside in Hampshire and Sussex. Rod Safe, the leading light in the club, had a museum of bicycles in Portsmouth and himself had several penny farthings and used to come on the rides on one of them but he was also a veteran car enthusiast and used to take part in the London to Brighton Run every year in his 1897 Benz. In addition to that he has a 1934 Morris 8 Series 1 Tourer. So cars and bicycles merge within the category of historic machinery. The interesting thing is the view of the world that we enthusiasts have. It is one that doesn't quite accept things as they are. We know that somehow or other our poor human family has gone off the rails and, to continue the metaphor, is careering perilously across the fields in a train designed to run on rails.

It was at one of the veteran cycle rallies at Chalk Pit Museum at Amberley in Sussex that one of the leading lights in the Club gave an interesting open air talk to the assembled crowd on the failure of governments in the 1950s to understand and organise the development of the motor car and consider some of the, he said, obvious side effects of mass motoring. He was not saying that governments should interfere with excessive rules and regulations, but that, when big changes are taking place, it is Government that should foresee some of the consequences which the average citizen might not anticipate. For example they

started to plan for a system of motorways and major dual car-
riageways between the big cities. The M1 was completed towards
the end of the decade. What they did not take into account was
the effect it would have within those cities. It not only changed
the cities but it also altered the way people lived. They were doing
things and going further than they had previously. Instead of
walking or cycling they jumped into the car. The long term effect
is that their health has become seriously damaged. Children who
once had to walk to school – I did – began to suffer from lack of
exercise and it has now grown into the massive problem of
obesity in children, which the Government is attempting to cope
with. I recently had to get my heart checked in St Thomas'
Hospital and it involved pedalling away on one of those stationary bicycles while the technician monitored the effects on a
screen. In conversation he pointed out to me how bad our state
of health was getting in Britain and in the developed countries
generally. It was now best in those Third World countries where
they had sufficient of the basic necessities of life but had to walk
or cycle to work every day. Interesting, I thought.

Our speaker, no doubt, had an axe to grind. He wanted a
world fit for cyclists to exercise themselves in. The problem he
told us in a small country like England, where motorways are
not really needed, is not quite the same as in continental Europe
or America. There with the vast distances across sparsely popu-
lated countryside there might be some justification for tolerat-
ing them. I met someone recently who told me that he had been
to one of the big industrial cities of Germany and was sitting at
dinner beside the chairman of BMW. He had learned earlier that
they were undertaking the task of building the public transport
system for the city. He expressed his surprise and said that he
thought BMW dealt with motor cars. The response he got was
that cars now are only for journeys between cities not within
them.

It follows I suppose that, if that is the case, for city people to
use their cars to drive to the supermarket is quite a serious

mistake. It would be far better for a few trucks and vans to carry the goods to the local shops instead of a vast number of cars clogging up the roads of our towns and cities, trying to make their way to the supermarkets. We are locked into a system that not only has clear traffic related disadvantages but also requires oil in vast quantities to ensure its very existence, as the body requires blood for its life. Any country that threatens our oil supply must be regarded as a 'rogue state' and ultimately, if necessary, be gone to war with to defend our vital national interest.

I find that underlying the thoughts of members of our very English 'old' car clubs there is an unconscious, and possibly not so unconscious, belief that there is something fundamentally wrong with the way our modern civilisation is moving. It is not just a nostalgic joy in the old and sentimental but a testimony to what could have been done with the motor car for the benefit of all, had not mass politics and mass motoring come to blight our lives. Imagine if the great and diverse range of car makers such as developed just before the First World War and continued for some time afterwards had been able to go on. How different things would be. A car would have been a long term investment. Families might have had one instead of half a dozen and the car would have been expected to last 20, 30 or even 50 years. Small workshops would be dotted across the country, where enthusiastic boys, and girls if they wanted to, would undergo a tough apprenticeship and come out with a sense of having achieved something worthwhile. How much better that would have been than having a large number of dropouts from phoney universities. And the principle applies to the whole range of honest trades which have engaged and employed the vast majority of mankind since the beginning of civilisation. Unfortunately, since the Industrial Revolution, the world has gone in a different direction. The car industry is simply a striking example of the insatiable greed of the few knocking out the many small car makers and incorporating them in their own motor manufacturing empires. Hamptons is one such example. It was gobbled up by the ever expanding Morris empire.

Another unfortunate effect of the car itself is the way in which it has accelerated the whole pace of life. Because we can get from place to place so rapidly and easily we get caught up in undertaking more and more things. I recall talking to a peripatetic music teacher in Southampton. She was breathless but had snatched a moment to tell me that she had seven different things to do that afternoon: two more lessons in other schools, a music teacher's committee meeting and a couple of private lessons in different parts of town and finally a concert to conduct in the Guildhall. All this she blamed on her car. Without it she would never have got herself involved in such breathless activity. And so much for music which is supposed to soothe and calm the human breast!

So the great misfortune in the nineteen-twenties was that motor manufacture was starting to be concentrated into very few hands and near monopolies of production were created. One cannot help thinking that in a more sensible world the great variety of small manufacturers with high grade skills, not just of cars but also of the various components, such as SU carburettors, would have had a far better chance of making for a far happier society. If nothing else the bitter conflicts between management and unions would have been far less likely to arise in such an industrial structure. But many would argue that to maintain that state of affairs would entail interference by governments in affairs in which they had no right to interfere. I do not know the answer, but I do know that there is one startling example of something like this in history. The Tudor Government under Henry VIII did intervene to stop Jack o' Newbury setting up a factory with 600 looms, which would have devastated the trade of a multitude of independent weavers. Looking back at history the consequences for the country seemed to have been highly beneficial.

What does also seem clear is that the process towards monopolisation that accelerated in the 1950s was clearly assisted by

government action, by interference on behalf of the motor manufacturers and by the wider vested interests of the Road Lobby.
Government did interfere. They did so on behalf of the giant car
empires, ostensibly in the name of the people. They changed the
timing of the issuing of new number plates to boost sales after
the Motor Show. They changed the law to allow cars to park on
urban roads at night without lights. I know it was said to be
done for the convenience of the motorist, and it was very convenient indeed, but it paved the way for an enormous increase
in the car population and the endless rows of parked cars we see
in our towns today. They encouraged the vast closure of railway
lines under Beeching and destroyed the heart of the public
transport system, making it almost impossible for vast numbers
of people to carry on their lives without the motor car. And this
was done at a time when a goodly proportion of them would
happily have avoided the expense and responsibility of running
a car. In America the idea was cleverly put around that what was
good for General Motors was good for America. It is slowly
dawning that that is not quite the case. The idea that the motor
industry was necessarily good for a country was the terrible
mistake of the twentieth century.

Chapter 5

Coleman's Car

Barrie Carter, who had a regular column in one of the classic car magazines, asked me to write about some of the episodes which were not included in my book, Coleman's Drive (my original publisher chose the title, not me). As I thought about it, it occurred to me that I had written the story about the journey but not – or only to a limited extent – about the car. It's time to do so here and very appropriate.

The story began before I actually got the car. I had had very many Austin Sevens I've lost count, but one single event was pivotal in deciding to set out on my journey to New York, although I didn't realise it at the time. I was at home on my parent's farm in Norfolk on vacation from the university and was wandering around the fields when my eyes caught sight of some rusty old iron in the ditch running beside the hedge (the best things in my life seem to have come out of ditches!). I investigated and quickly the familiar form of an A7 chassis revealed itself to me. I wanted a few bits off it and as much of it was very rusty and we didn't value old iron, even in the shape of an Austin Seven chassis, in those days, and as I didn't have a welding torch to burn it off, I set about it with a sledge hammer. I got what I wanted in the end but the struggle convinced me that this was surely from a car that was tough enough to withstand any amount of battering. The second great attraction of the Austin 7 was its size. I could almost lift it out of trouble single-handed, I thought, but I hadn't reckoned with the midday sun in the Atacama Desert when picking up a spanner was almost beyond my physical ability. The third was the little Austin's maddening tendency to be always pretending to be about to go wrong while almost never actually doing so. I can't help believing that Austin cunningly thought this up as a way of keeping drivers on their toes and alert! Anyway, these thoughts had quite an influence on me when the idea of finding a way to get to the Inca remains in Peru seriously began to exercise my mind. I couldn't think of doing what that great horseman, Aimé Tschaiffley, did with his horses, but could I do it with an Austin 7? The idea had dawned on me and it rattled about in my mind for many years in my twenties.

Now I need to introduce the car itself, perhaps just the car. MO6320 was just a poor discarded baby Austin which had been used by the owner of a rowing-boat business at Port Meadow on the banks of the Thames just outside Oxford. I often used to walk over the fields when I was at the university at the beginning of the 1950s and there was always a fair chance that I would see it pulling a rowing boat up the bank and across the meadow without any kind of trailer, just sliding over the grass or mud. I developed the kind of respect for it that you would for any car that did such an amazing job for its owner, but beyond that, I thought it wasn't worth thinking about. Just leave it to its labour – probably eternally. Then a year or two later after I'd left the university and was preparing to earn my own living as a teacher I went back to Oxford to visit friends and one day in the late Autumn I went for a walk over the familiar meadow. In the back of my mind I thought I might see the little car, but no. There was not a sign of it, but as I walked away along a ditch I caught sight of something in the undergrowth that looked as if it might be interesting. Yes, it was the little car minus the engine – a hood and windscreen it never had. Immediately I went back to see if I could find the owner of the boatyard. This was serious. What had happened, I asked him. 'Oh,' he said, 'I broke a half-shaft in the back axle so I took out the engine which might come in useful for one of my boats and slung away the rest.' Anyway to cut a long story short, he told me I could have the car but he wanted two pounds ten shillings for the engine. I fixed the deal straightaway. We pulled the car out of the ditch, set it upright and I took off the back-axle, an easy job on an Austin Seven as it is only bolted on to the ends of two quarter elliptical springs (incidentally one of the factors that makes the cornering of the Austin 7 a little odd since, on bends, one side of the back-axle stretches out a little further than the other). I removed the rear seat of the Austin Seven I was driving at the time, shoved the back-axle in and a day or two later headed for London.

At this point I should explain that second-hand cars were fetching prohibitive prices. There was a two year waiting list for new cars, but by paying ten times the list price – if you were lucky – you could jump the queue. In the post-war period nothing that ran on wheels fetched much under £300 – even very humble Austin 7s. So I had got a car for what now would be called £2.50, but that was not the end of the tale.

By this time my family had moved back to South London where I grew up and an old coach house at the bottom of the garden served as an excellent garage. It had a little room up some rickety stairs for the coachman to sleep in, excellent for storing spare parts. I carried the back-axle up there and got it ready to work on and round about the same time managed to pick up a couple of half-shafts from a breaker's yard. One I put aside and the other I fitted into the back-axle. It all went quite smoothly, at least I thought so.

The next thing was to trundle back to Oxford and just fit the axle back on the car and pop the engine into place and tow the lot back to London. The weather was getting cold and wet by now and when I went out on the meadow although it was not actually raining it was certainly very muddy and cold.

Altogether it was a pretty unforgettable experience putting the back-axle on and just slotting the engine and gear box into place. I did it very roughly and didn't even attempt to get the car running but simply left it ready for towing. Christmas was approaching and I couldn't find a friend to come down with me until after the holiday. When I did eventually go in early January the frosts, severe in the days before global warming interrupted our normal weather, rose only a few degrees nearer to zero in the daytime. My friend Dick Thomas drove my Austin back and I sat in my new acquisition with no hood or windscreen. It was another rather memorable journey. However, I told myself that soldiers in the First World War endured far worse for much longer with the added disadvantage of grenades and bullets whizzing round their heads. I should count myself lucky, and in any case, all's well that ends well: MO6320 was sitting proudly in the old coach house and I felt all the exhilaration you might expect if you'd just climbed Everest. I let things rest until the warmer weather. In the meantime I managed to pick up a windscreen and when spring seemed to have come I started work in earnest. I fixed the engine, the gear box, the starter and hey ho even the magneto worked and produced an excellent spark to make the by now unrationed petrol do its job. I thought I'd try it out slyly on the road. It was fine going up the short driveway. The trouble came when I tried to get it into second gear. It wouldn't go in and it wasn't simply that it didn't have syncromesh. I knew Austin Seven gear boxes well and if you took your time you hardly needed to double clutch up or down. I was puzzled for some time. Slowly it dawned on me that something was really wrong. How about going backwards and seeing what happened? Then I changed into the next gear. Hey presto, it went backwards beautifully and into top and it went even faster. But as I didn't feel like going on a long journey like that I drove it straight back into the coach house. I quickly realised that I'd fitted the back-axle the wrong way round and in the cold and mud out on the meadow I wasn't concerned about anything much except getting the bits bolted together and towable.

I split the axle, put the crown wheel and half-shaft in from the other side and bolted it all up again and could hardly wait to try it out. Out on the road I went into second gear, then into top and felt it a pity to aim at anything less than John o' Groats. I thought it seemed magnificent. I called a friend, now a doctor but then near the end of his medical training and told him that my Austin was running beautifully, no matter that it didn't have a hood and the brakes were dodgy. There was no MOT in those days and there wasn't much difference between brakes that worked and brakes that didn't – on an Austin Seven. My friend said that a girl we knew was having a very smart 21st birthday party up in Hertfordshire on the following Saturday, could we go up in the car? I reluctantly said I suppose so. In those days you just put a cheque for £3.50 or whatever it was for a quarter's licence in an envelope and off you went and sometimes you didn't even bother posting it until you got back but you made sure you had the letter in your pocket to show the police if necessary. I'd been done twice for brakes and each time had a fine of ten shillings. I didn't worry too much about that because usually you didn't get stopped if nothing drew the attention of the police. The system in those days was that the policeman asked you to get in the car and apply your brakes so you pushed on the brake peddle with all your might. If he could push the car easily you might get booked but if he detected some resistance he would suggest that the brakes might be improved with some adjustment, and you smiled and said 'Thank you officer I shall attend to that straightaway.' Our consciences didn't trouble us too much. We may have been a little economic with the law but we always paid our licence fee if we kept the car on the road and remembered that Sir Herbert Austin always claimed that good brakes made bad drivers.

Anyway Saturday arrived and it was pouring with rain and my friend and another rather smartly dressed young man who was with him at the London Hospital arrived on my doorstep. I don't think they had quite appreciated that the car had no hood and certainly no side screens and that little bit of quick thinking was needed. My friend suggested that a large umbrella might be the answer, which they had with them and which evoked my uneasy agreement. We could go fairly slowly, I thought, but feared that we might make ourselves a bit conspicuous to the police. However, it was raining and there seemed to be no alternative to the umbrella with the edge of it kept just below the top of the windscreen plus keeping the speed down to about twenty miles an hour. I hadn't taken into account the fact that the suction windscreen wiper was not connected and therefore was not operating. Fortunately there was a small lever on it which enabled the driver to operate it by hand. This I did, but what with the unstable umbrella, the lack of brakes and the wet roads, driving was none too easy, but it was all right so long as no unexpected hazard occurred. I knew it was up to me to maintain such keen observation ahead that it didn't.

We got to the party without any serious incidents but with patches of wet on the extremities of our best clothes. We weren't in fancy dress but I suspected that the guests who saw us arrive gained the impression that the Austin was! A pleasant, rather proper evening was enjoyed by all, even me in spite of my slight foreboding about the return journey. Although there was no drinking and driving law at that time I was pretty careful with the alcohol. I had rigged up the two small front lights to work directly from the battery, as well as the single little rear light, which was all the law then required. I knew I was going to have to strain my eyes all the way back to get a vague idea of the outline of the road ahead. It was all right though. I had had considerable experience of the dense fogs that characterised November in those days. The Chummy had the advantage that you could flip up the top half of the windscreen to get a direct view of the road ahead. Fortunately the rain had subsided by then and we had a relatively good journey home. I hadn't thought of going to South America then but I realised later that it was experiences like that which were a jolly good preparation for the trip from Buenos Aires to new York.

Later I was working at a special school in Hampshire for severely disturbed children. It was a terrible strain and was a more or less a twenty-four hour a day job in term time. I always thought that my slightly unbalanced frame of mind was responsible for the idea of going to South America in the first place. My parents were moving and the coach house had to be cleared. The Austin Chummy was in it. It had to be found a home. There was an open garage at the school which I kept my Morris in and there was room for the Chummy, but I wondered if the bigger boys would regard it with the respect I considered it deserved. Fortunately at the back of the garage there was a narrow doorway into a room with a bench in it, not unlike the upper room in the coach house. It was obvious I was not going to get the Chummy through it. It also seemed obvious to me that there was only one way to do it and that was by dismantling the car, taking off the front and back axles and removing the windscreen, then by turning the body on its side it could be humped in. And the bits could follow it. I took the engine out and set it up on the bench ready to strip down and rebuild, even though I was too short of money to buy all the new parts I should have liked to have fitted. Perhaps that turned out to be just as well as slightly worn parts operate more freely in extreme conditions. Around this time another almost miraculous stroke of luck occurred. I went into a very small yard behind a shop in Southampton, where I found the pram-type hood fitted on to the pre-1926 Austin Sevens, a very rare item indeed.

I should have mentioned two amusing incidents which might have altered the course of my life before I went down to Hampshire. At one point I decided to sell the poor little Chummy. People remarked to me that an old Austin 7 would only be interesting if it had been made before 1925. The prototype was constructed in 1922. Some hand-made models were made after that and the assembly lines were set up and ran in

1925. Mine, said people with pretensions about the history of old cars, was not worth keeping. I weakened and advertised it for fifty pounds. The days of the very high prices were receding and most people looked down their noses at Austin 7s. I shall never forget a very nice girl responded to my advert. She was pretty keen but only offered me forty pounds. We haggled over it. She went up to forty-five pounds and I still said no and she accused me of being like 'the Rock of Gibraltar'. I suppose, looking back, there was something inside me that didn't want to part with it, although I did later sell it to friend who was going to learn to drive. I remember driving her to a local laundrette with a huge pile of washing in the back. I think she somehow got the idea on the way that this wasn't really the ideal car for her to learn on. I had to agree and gave her money back. Destiny seemed to decide that this was my car and no one else's!

By the beginning of 1959 I'd done quite a bit of work on various parts of the car and I thought I'd pretend to take the idea of going to South America seriously. So I started writing to a variety of firms to see if they would sponsor me. Austin was obviously the first firm to approach and I got a nice reply saying that they were very interested in the idea but as they received about twenty such requests a week they had to say no. Castrol were fairly scathing and said that unless I was supported by an expensive advertising campaign in the United States I was very unlikely to get any publicity that would be of use to them. The editor of the Geographical Magazine told me in a letter that he'd crossed the Andes in very powerful car and only just made it. In an Austin 7 it would be impossible. When I returned from my trip and told him I'd done it, he replied, 'I still believe it's impossible.' The only real encouragement came from Arthur Savage of the Board of Trade. He thought it a great idea and, if I succeeded, it would boost the reputation of British goods.

By this time I saw clearly that a change of tack was badly needed and also by this time that second hand cars had become much less expensive. I not only had a few hundred pounds saved but I also had a really nice 18 month old Morris Minor Tourer which I was sure I could sell for a few hundred more. I reckoned I was in a position to finance the expedition myself. This had an electrifying effect. Austin said they would undertake to get and send out any spares I needed to any part of my route wherever and whenever I needed them. Dunlop heaped new sets of tyres on me. Shell promised to ask their marketing companies in the main cities on the way to look after me and cover the cost of fuel to the next stage. In fact they usually doubled my own estimate. In addition, small parts came tumbling in daily. The trick had worked except on one point: my own finances seemed precariously inadequate. Quite unexpectedly I received a letter from the manager of the Royal Mail Lines asking me to come up and see him in London. I can hardly describe the final preparations without mentioning this crucial meeting. Briefly he said they had decided to take my car to Buenos Aires for a nominal charge of £18 though they would have to charge the full third class fare on top, of £93. Suddenly, at a stroke almost, the whole fantasy became not only possible, but somehow inescapable. I went to bed that night wondering what in the name of fate I'd let myself in for. I had some pretty ugly dreams that night and the preparations took on a new urgency.

The final preparation of the car involved using expanding rings rather than having the engine rebored and fitting new pistons, a deliberate choice for reasons already mentioned. I put Molyspeed on every moving component of the car except the brakes. My father had been with Elliott Automation before it came on to the open market, who used molybdenum disulphide in machinery destined for tropical countries. Earlier they had carried out a test which greatly impressed my father. A car was chosen as a guinea pig and Molyspeed was added to the engine oil. After running the engine for long enough to distribute it to all the working parts the sump plug was removed and all the oil drained out. They then drove the car for seventy miles before the engine seized up! Having witnessed it himself, my father was so impressed that he used to bring home bottles of it for his own car and he always let me have some and encouraged me to use it. I've been addicted to it ever since. I used Barsleak in the radiator, which Mr D.H Piper (we didn't use Christian names for everybody in those days), the head of the Cord Piston Ring Company, told me they had just brought out and was so successful that Ford decided to put it into the radiators of all their new cars. Its effectiveness, despite all the overheating, was proved for me by my 'Drive'.

So the car was sprayed and checked by the workshop in Beaulieu and was– keep my fingers crossed– ready. Anything further would have to be done in South America and I could forget about all my anxieties for a few weeks.

My drive in the chummy from Buenos Aires to New York, going over the Andes into Chile, through the Atacama Desert, the jungles further north and then through Central America and finally into the USA, is another story and fills another book, *Coleman's Drive.*

Chapter 6

The Morris Minor Phase

In reality I suppose this phase really began back in 1949 when I drove our friends' new Morris. More accurately perhaps that was when the first germ of an idea that the Morris Minor was first set in the deep recesses of my mind as the post-War equivalent of the Austin Seven and the essence of all the post-War cars to follow. The talking point of the day was independent front suspension and the Minor was supposed to have had a horizontally opposed engine that would have made it go like a Jowett Javelin, that is to say, like a rocket. The black Morris Tourer, that I had just prior to setting out on my journey in South America, was the first realisation of my dream but it was overshadowed by the Chummy and the vision of it conquering the Andes and chugging through the deserts and jungles of the Southern hemisphere. It was only when I returned to earth, or rather to England, that a not too expensive, second-hand Morris Minor seemed the only thing that made sense. I ran round in the little Chummy for a month or two visiting friends. In what else could I arrive at their doors? The offer of $30,000 from the Yankee who wanted to hang it over the entrance to his mobile home park made a new popular car seem a tu'penny ha'penny thing beside the £10,000 Chummy. £500 then bought you a new Mini. My mind was made up. The car that had almost become part of me for nearly a year was destined for the Montagu Motor Museum.

So while I was making my delightful but inescapable social visits I kept my eyes open for an inexpensive Morris Minor and found a 1949 Tourer which seemed to suit me and my pocket very well despite the underpowered side-valve engine. Anyway what was a slightly underpowered engine beside what I had become daily accustomed to? It was maroon and perfectly satisfactory. Nevertheless I had to get a job as I couldn't live for ever on the little fortune I'd picked up on the trip. I moved into a hotel, Oakmore House Hotel, at Fairoak just outside Southampton. Wonderful old houses were going for next to nothing in those days and its owner, Ron Harris, had bought it and had a ready made hotel. Most of its residents were pretty regular. One or two were commercial travellers but they also included a number of the staff of Southern Television. Best of all was the fact that not only were there plenty of unused outbuildings, but there was also a fine five or six hundred yard drive. I didn't fail to see the potential of both. Not far away in the village was the Aburg Engineering workshop, who among other things raced Mini Coopers and were super engineers. By some quirk of circumstances they had a 1929 Square-nosed Morris Tourer with the 11.4 HP Hotchkiss engine, which had been brought up from Devon and had only travelled 29,000 miles in the whole of its life. This caught my fancy. It wasn't much good to Aburg as it was the very last car in the world which was suitable for racing. With a great effort a bare 40 mph could be forced out of it. 30 or 35 was it natural cruising speed – but what a ride! You really felt more than a cut above the little insignificant insects that were flashing past you at 45 or 50 miles an hour. It really was not for Aburg and I bought it for some reasonably low price. I oiled it and greased it. There was really very little to do to it. The paintwork was a little faded but that only added to its feeling of originality. The door catches were tight and unworn as were most things about it. The big artillery wheels were delightful. Cars didn't have to be MOT'd in those days but you did have to have an engineer's certificate to get an elderly car insured. I took it to a very reputable garage in Southampton and it received its certificate without any difficulty, which amounted to a lists of 'no appreciable wear and tear' and 'excellents'. I remember driving it down to Beaulieu when Michael Sedgwick was curator. 'Let me try it,' he said. 'Of course,' I replied, and typically he disappeared and didn't return until about two hours later. It really got the thumbs up when he did. Meanwhile the little maroon Minor was proving a trusty servant. I did very little to it except use it.

John Wickes was the transmission controller at Southern Television, who took the job after a very successful spell of acting and at that time was one of the permanent guests at Oakmore House. There was an element of the theatrical in his relation to his car, an early Vauxhall Victor with the gear change on the steering column and only three forward gears. The paint on the roof was wearing a little thin and patches of undercoat, blotches really, were evident. John didn't feel inclined to spend his hard earned money from Southern Television respraying an old Vauxhall and hit on the idea of painting it with glue and throwing sand at it. Two tone cars were fashionable at this period. There was much discussion about how successful it would be but John stuck to his plan and it didn't turn out at all badly. The next scheme that his success inspired did involve considerable expenditure. He took the car round to Val Gardiner at Aburg, a highly experienced engineer at making cars go. Twin carbs, raising the compression ratio and smoothing the exhaust ports together with twin exhaust pipes were the outcome, and pretty effective it was, too. John had the idea that he wanted his car to be like 'A wolf in sheep's clothing', to use his own original expression from the discussions before the job was done: a dowdy old Vauxhall with a highly unusual roof that could suddenly hare off like a Ferrari.

What a contrast it was beside my lumbering old Cowley, which really was a sturdy old ox in ox's clothing. Nevertheless as time went on, and somewhat affected by the experience of John's rocket-like potential, I grew a little dissatisfied with the performance of the side valve engine in the Minor. Pat Goldacre, who had briefly owned my Chummy and decided to buy my red Y-Model Ford, paid a visit one weekend to Oakmore House and determined that she would like to move one more rung up the car ownership ladder as soon as I could find something else to replace the Minor. The something else of course had to be a Minor and certainly of the touring variety. I found an approximation to what I had in mind in the form of a rather baldly resprayed, powder-blue tourer with the BMC overhead valve A Type engine borrowed from the Austin A 30. I dared not try rubbing down the paintwork in case the undercoat, or even the metal, began to show. It served me quite well. Of course it had the larger raised headlamps and the engine that did quite well in the lighter Austin but was still inadequate in the Minor. I never, however, entertained any special affection for it. In contrast its successor, a beautiful white tourer, seemed to me almost my ideal. It also had the 1,000 cc engine and whistled along smoothly and merrily. We went twice to Hamburg in it, once when my daughter was a baby. A carrycot and all the necessary baby things fitted quite comfortably on the back seat and I don't recall a single mechanical problem on those two long journeys. When my son was born it soon became clear that a more spacious vehicle was called for. Letting it go was quite a wrench.

I've missed out another story, which chronologically fitted in prior to the Hamburg journeys. I had been searching for a bungalow or cottage in Hampshire, out in the country because that was all I could hope to afford on a teacher's salary – and after a great deal of hunting I found a dairyman's cottage at Hoe Gate, near Hambledon. It had water and it had electricity and not much else: no bathroom and a shed in the garden for a WC. But the price was right, at least it was vaguely within my price range. I might just possibly be able to scrape together £1,350. I managed to get the agent to negotiate a reduction of £100 so I set about raising the money. Mortgages on anything but a fairly well kept property with all mod cons were impossible to obtain. It irritated us at the time but we didn't realise that it was one of the factors keeping the prices of property down. I had a rather nice Hillman Minx convertible with the gear change on the steering column, a very smart feature in those days, so the first thing to do was to see what I could raise for that. I advertised it and got £250. There was an old Standard 8 with a noisy back axle lying about at my parent's home, so I settled on that as a temporary measure, as a car was an inescapable necessity if I was going to live out in the wilds. One day I might get back to a Minor but at that time a cottage seemed like the fulfilment of a wonderful dream and scarcely any sacrifice was not too great. I managed to borrow £500 from the bank and my kind friends in Dorset lent me another £500. I was there with just a steady repayable debt. A builder whose daughter I taught helped me put in a bathroom and a cesspit at a modest cost and that, with a lot of hard work, gradually enabled me to turn a 300-year-old flint and brick cottage into a simple but very acceptable habitation.

The dream lasted for a few years but eventually we decided to move nearer to Southampton and by now I could think of myself as a real home owner. The cottage had gone up considerably in value and we decided to buy a new house next to John Wickes of Vauxhall Victor fame, who by now was also married. It was not hard to get a mortgage this time and I often think how lucky I was compared to young people today. So everything went quite smoothly. There was a good big garden and ample space for a garage. I had started with one of the earlier Travellers with the engine borrowed from the Austin A30, but it was clearly underpowered, so I moved up to the Minor 1000 Traveller with a very good body but a rather worn engine which I rebuilt from scratch in my new garage.

The engine was a huge success from the word go and boosted my confidence as an engine rebuilder even further. My son, Kai, who was only two years old at the time took a great interest in what I was doing and in the Traveller generally. He loved to stand in the driving seat and start the engine up. On one occasion the car was standing on the slight incline of the driveway with the brake only lightly on. He started the engine, released the brake whereupon the car started to move. Immediately his hands left the steering wheel and he threw his arms up in the air and exclaimed, 'I've done it, I've done it!'

The car gave many years' excellent service round England and Scotland and one or two trips abroad but no spectacularly long trips, except one. I had bought an elderly 10ft caravan which was considerably heavier than the modern caravans of the time. It was rather pleasant and luxurious inside. I had fixed a tow bar onto the Traveller and taken it on a few holidays in England, including one or two in the Isle of Wight. Friends sometimes laughed at the idea of pulling a caravan with a Minor but I stuck to my view that if you use your gears right a Minor will pull almost anything. As a schoolteacher you don't have too much money but you do have nice long holidays in the Summer. So we decided to camp in the South of France and away we went down that same route I'd travelled on what I can only describe as that awful holiday in 1957. This time it was punctuated by a stop at Lille for a few days at the home of the French assistant at my school, Suzanne, who used sometimes to visit us at home and who had become a great friend of the children and of my wife. Her family owned a brewery in Lille where she had grown up with eleven brothers and sisters. It was fortunate that we had stopped as Alice, my daughter, got ill and we had to call in a French doctor who dealt with her problem very quickly and effectively. We were ready to go and arranged to meet Suzanne under the Eiffel Tower at 3 o'clock on the day of our return. The caravan swayed rather perilously, especially on downhill sections of the route, but I soon learned how to arrange the weight in the caravan to cure that. On our return journey we stayed at one of those excellent camp sites which almost every French town seems to have. The French certainly know how to organise themselves for holidays. Ours had been a great success and we made good friends with a Danish and a German couple. The German had been an airline pilot who had been involved in the training of pilots and I remember discussing the subject. The Germans, he said, tried to base their teaching on too many rules. The Americans were inclined to be too haphazard, but the British brought the trainees to the very edge of disaster and brought them out safely. As a result their pilots, he considered, were the best at coping with emergencies. Living near the Air Training College I found this opinion particularly interesting. We left the Danes promising that we would meet them one day in Denmark but unfortunately never met that promise.

As I had learnt to balance the weight in the caravan I was able to pull it at fair speeds up the long stretches of the Routes Nationales of France on our return journey. After only one night's stop at a campsite we set off early in the morning on the road to Paris with our 3 o'clock goal firmly in mind. It was on this leg of the journey that we came near to disaster. The roads then on the whole were very good but they did have the odd pothole here and there. Our heavily loaded car and caravan obviously felt the bumps once or twice but there didn't seem too much need to worry until suddenly the French motorists started hooting disconcertingly, not one but all who were driving along that road. Time, I thought, to have a glance in my mirror and I saw smoke coming out from the offside wheel arch and I knew it was time to pull up without delay. When I got out I saw immediately that the wheel had splayed out and was rubbing against the wooden wheel arches of the caravan, which were smouldering and about to burst into flame. Further inspection revealed that the axle beam had broken in two about a foot in from the wheel. It was obviously a front axle from a car made before independent suspension became universal and adapted for the caravan. By a stroke of luck I could just see what looked like a garage a quarter of a mile or so up the road and there was only one thing to do: disconnect the caravan, install the family in it and drive up to get help. The idea of our rendezvous at 3 o'clock now seemed beyond the bounds of possibility. I tried to explain my problem in my very bad French. It was then about eleven o'clock. They came out with rope and tackle, took a look at the axle and quickly decided to clamp and rope it together. When it was done they indicated that they thought it would be safe to reconnect the caravan and tow it very slowly to their workshop. Once there they phoned the local branch of John Deere, the agricultural merchants, and arranged for them to pick up the axle and weld it together again. They whipped the axle off in double quick time. Meantime they took the family into a very pleasant little garden at the side of the garage where we fixed ourselves up with a picnic lunch and relaxed in comfort. Soon John Deere arrived and went off with the axle to deal with it in their workshop with the heavy welding equipment used for welding farm machinery. An hour or so later they returned with the axle in one beautifully welded piece. In next to no time the garage had the axle fitted back on to the caravan and ready to drive off. I wondered where else in the world one could find such efficiency? I might now say in some of the out of the way places in South America, equal but not better service. Soon we were on the road to Paris and, miracle of miracles, we kept our appointment, hardly an hour late! The most satisfying aspect of the episode, in retrospect, was that just before leaving Dover the AA were arranging insurances for caravans for a pound and I bought one. As a result all the labour and transporting of the axle didn't cost me a penny. We met Suzanne who was waiting patiently and drove out to the campsite where she had left her little Renault 4. So all's well that ends well. I recall that we had a delicious dinner in Paris and set out for Calais on the following morning after staying at the campsite beside the ferry terminal. An early morning boat got us into Dover as the sun was rising and we had a hearty British breakfast for 3/6d – 1/6d for the children. It was the last long journey with that caravan but not quite the end of the story. Although the car's gearbox gave no trouble on the journey, the strain had been a bit too much for it and it broke down some months later. The answer came in the form of a second hand box from the breakers. I was always quite happy with engines but wary about gear boxes.

The car went on for several years and as the MOT had been introduced by then I took it into the Lowford Garage near my school, where John Kearley was the workshop manager and he did the test and any small jobs necessary to get it through as well as spraying it with oil underneath every year. Then one year I took it in and when I returned I saw John looked unhappy about it. 'You've got serious problems. The rust is pretty bad. It'll go on for another year but by then it won't be economic to do any more welding.' Sadly I decided to part with it shortly afterwards. John left the Lowford Garage and I didn't see him again for some years.

When I was in New York at the end of my American trip I stayed with Franklin Kosig who was working at the United Nations and had an early Volvo. A funny shape I thought but a wonderful ride. I wished that the British motor industry had decided to emulate the quality of Volvo through their whole range of cars instead of trying to compete with the cheaper continentals. We could have swept the board and perhaps the world might have gone in for quality rather than quantity. As I went around I came across a really nice 1600 Volvo saloon. It wasn't a traveller but it did have a really large boot and as it was pretty spacious inside, it would be quite satisfactory for the family. The Swedes were known for their thorough treatment against rust – they had to be in their climate – and that was a sore point with the new British cars at the time. I told myself that I could think of it as a larger version of the Morris Minor, and in many ways it was similar in broad layout in spite of still having a 6 volt electrical system. It gave excellent service for a year or two and then I saw a Volvo 144S that not only had twin carbs and gave a fantastic performance – I took it up to almost 130 mph once on an empty motorway – but also was red and rather dashing. I remember Michael Goldacre always referred to it as my 'millionaire's car'. The children didn't like the Volvos, however. They said they made them sick and demonstrated it! 'Why can't we go back to Morris Minors?' they asked.

In 1975 the Referendum on the Common Market was coming up. I was on the 'No' side and someone stuck a note on my windscreen saying: 'Why don't you have a British car?' The Allegro had just come out, in 1973 to be exact, and the idea of returning to the name of Austin had very great appeal. I asked Vic Mant, the Senior Master at my school, whose son had a garage just outside Southampton, if he could get me one. 'If you must have an Allegro, I suppose I can,' he scoffed. In fact he got me two over the course of time. The first had one or two problems but I thought it fairly satisfactory. I couldn't help thinking they were getting a rather unfair reputation. Then only months later I got a message from my reluctant salesman to say that he had an almost new Allegro at a very reasonable price. It was 'N reg' and only a few months old and seemed too good to miss. It developed a little problem with the alternator at first, but that I thought was not the car's fault. The same brand of alternator was fitted on to a whole variety of modern cars. I had also at about this time arranged, more accurately Michael Perry, my solicitor friend, had arranged to exchange the cottage I still had at Hambledon – I'd let it to a couple who loved it dearly and who over the years I thought of as friends rather than tenants – for the four story house I now have in Vauxhall, London. It had been vandalised and the windows were covered with corrugated iron. The Allegro with its roof rack carried endless superfluous sheets of corrugated iron down to Southampton and masses of interesting building materials up to London. It served me magnificently for several years. It had 4,000 miles on the clock when I bought it and 120,000 when I sold it for not far short of what I had originally paid. Not bad, I thought. It was the end of that Allegro as far as I was concerned, but not quite the end of the Allegro story.

It was at this juncture that I had a rather unpleasant operation and after seeing the Local Education Authority's doctor decided to take early retirement and a new chapter in the motor car saga was about to begin.

Chapter 7

Twilight Motoring

My teaching career had been rather intermittent and that together with retiring early meant that my pension would be very small indeed. That, however, didn't worry me very much as I rather relished the idea of 'living lightly'. I had let a part of my house to a couple, with whom I had become good friends. David had an old and rather dilapidated Morris Minor saloon, which he sold me for £20. I recall a few beautiful Summer afternoons when I had it out on the lawn beside the apple tree. I went over everything and gave it a good servicing. I jacked it up and had a good look underneath. When I felt a bit tired or exasperated, I took a short rest under the cool of the tree to recover or reflect on some mechanical problem. I don't think I ever enjoyed messing about with a car so much as I did that Summer. That settled my transport problems now that the Allegro had gone. I rather liked the idea that if it got dented it was just a matter of a hammer and a spot of paint to put it right. None of your professional panel beating and expensive respraying for me, I thought. I just wanted a workhorse and that was exactly what I got. I'm afraid that my children were more than a little ashamed of it, but they had asked me to buy a Morris Minor whenever they felt sick in the Volvo or the Allegro. The car ran quite well but it was rather tatty in almost every respect. Nevertheless I liked it. It was like an old pair of threadbare slippers with holes in them and threads hanging loose everywhere, for which age and familiarity breed a special attachment. The engine was rather worn but, more significant, the clutch was prone to slip occasionally and grew progressively worse.

One sunny afternoon as I was driving back to London the clutch gave up the ghost altogether. So I decided I'd have the engine out and do the job properly and use it to teach my son, Kai, about engines. He was tremendously enthusiastic and that was great fun. We got a new clutch plate and did all the usual things to the engine: rebore, new pistons and valves, etc. The day came to fit the clutch plate and put the whole shoot back in the car. All went well until the moment came to start it up. I was getting in and out of the car and pointing things out like a good teacher and hadn't noticed that the oil warning switch was not connected. I failed to look properly at the warning light, put my hand in to pull the starter button. It started almost instantly to our great delight. I looked in at the warning light, which I thought had gone out because the engine had fired. I assumed that the oil was circulating until I heard a nasty noise and quickly turned it off. The engine ran when I got the oil moving but we knew that the damage had been done and our delight was very severely dented indeed. I discovered my error and 'better late than never' proceeded to put it right. Although the engine was never up to the standard I expected, it did run for some years and Alice learned to drive in it, making it a little more acceptable to her sensibilities. My children were growing up and I was growing old – or at least beginning to. It seemed to me that there was a sudden leap from not being quite grown up into old age. The sense of being truly grown up and responsible seemed to me to be something that had simply eluded me and I wasn't altogether sure I was sorry. Ambition, at least in the sense in which one is supposed to build up a solid career, had always seemed to me a bit of a curse. I liked following every path life offered, but I liked to take them all with a pinch of salt. Life should be a tapestry into which you weave all sorts of shapes and patterns and upon which you always look back in surprise and wonder. 'Did I really do that?' I often asked myself about my journey in South America.

Obviously I had to have some kind of transport while I was working on the Minor and it was at this point that a Fiat 800 presented itself for next to nothing. The MOT was nearing its end but at least I thought it would cover me while we were working on the engine. It did. And when the MOT ran out I took it up to Frank in Islington, who ran a firm called Minifix. Frank was a real find. I saw quite by chance a notice on the side of the road pointing up to his 'works', so out of curiosity I went up the narrow alley way and found Frank with a couple of young chaps and an elderly Mini, explaining carefully what they had to do to get it through the MOT. He was being really helpful and I thought what a pleasant attitude, and when I was talking to him after they had gone he said to me, 'We try to follow the spirit of the law here, not the letter. We want to see safe cars on the road'. My first impressions seemed to be well and truly confirmed. I was to discover he was always like that and I always brought my cars up to him for the test even though it was somewhat out of my way. He would fail cars if he felt that something was dangerous even if it was not strictly within the MOT requirements and he would turn a blind eye to little things that didn't really matter. You always felt you would get fairly treated and you knew that if he failed a car it would be for good reasons. He was generous about slight wear on bearings and joints when he was sure they would be quite safe for another year. He always did small jobs and counted them within the cost of the MOT, but was fairly expensive for major repairs. So in due course I took the Fiat to him to see what his opinion would be. He passed it but said it would not last more than another year without excessive expense. When the Minor was ready for the road again I took the Fiat over to the Isle of Wight and kept it beside my caravan to use whenever I went there. I was thus able to leave my usual car at Lymington. As I had an open insurance policy I merely had to tax it for the summer months.

The Minor did great work for many years carrying building materials to my house in London and collecting all sorts of things from skips by the roadside. It was a period when people were throwing away things that have since become very fashionable. You found traditional doors, brass knobs and interesting fittings there for the collecting and collect them I did. There was not a lot of room inside the Minor but the roof rack was invariably piled high. My house was a derelict old off-licence which had previously been a merchant's warehouse so rebuilding it inside with what people threw away was fascinating, but that really is another story.

When the Fiat's year was nearly up I brought it back from the Island and gave it to Kai. To start with he drove it on the lawn, which was fairly large, round and round in circles – not to the benefit of the lawn – but certainly to the benefit of his driving and engineering experience, despite the frequent pleas: 'Can I have some more petrol, Dad?' My spare can was always being emptied. We were on the edge of a network of private roads going up to the beach and passing through farms and fields. After asking the police if it was legal I first used to go with him on those bumpy tracks, but later let him go on his own. He could travel for several miles and was often away for hours on end. He sometimes used to take a boy from the nearby cottages for company and, despite my strict instructions that he should only drive the car himself, he let his friend have a go with unfortunate results: he drove it onto a heap of gravel and crashed the whole underneath of the poor car—it was not hard to see why Frank had said that it would not last for more than another year! The pair of them returned on foot pretty crest-fallen and I had to go out with a tow-rope and attempt to pull the wreck back home. I succeeded and gave the remains to a local breaker. Now that Kai was driving quite well I sometimes cheered him up by taking him out to a disused airfield in the New Forest and letting him drive the Morris Minor. It was fine on the old concrete runway and reminded me of the day I took my own driving test, but there was no way I was going to let him drive it for hours on end on the local stony tracks.

It was hard for a young chap of 14 or so, who had learnt to drive pretty competently, not to have a decent bit of driving at weekends – except with his Dad. I had heard of someone locally who had a couple of 105E Fords – the model with the rear window slanting the wrong way – in his back yard, and so we went to investigate. They had both failed their MOTs and were not cars which at that time attracted the interest of enthusiasts. They were not nearly antique enough. We could have which one we liked for a tenner, so we settled on the one we liked best. The mechanics were perfectly OK and were to prove rather more than OK, but the body had fair bit of rust in it. It served its purpose well and whenever anything went wrong Kai showed his developing skill in tackling it. The only downside was that I had to be rather careful about retrieving my tools and although he soon learnt to build up a collection of his own – there was no difficulty deciding on Christmas presents for him at that period – it was sometimes a matter of dispute who owned which.

In the meantime I was feeling the need for a car on the Isle of Wight and as luck would have it some friends had a little Fiat 500 they wanted to get rid of. A bit of work and an overhaul of the brakes by John Kearley, a wizard with hydraulic brakes, and Hey Presto it passed its MOT, at Frank's, of course. It really was a lovely little car to have on the Island – almost too good. It had often crossed my mind that it would be a wonderful idea to have two identical Morris Minors: one to keep on the Island and just take the licence disc backwards and forwards. How tempting it was: just one licence, one insurance and just one Minor would have to be MOT'd for both. Fortunately my law abiding side got the better of me and I was very happy with the Fiat, though as I left it on a public road near the ferry, sometimes for weeks on end, I did find a notice from the Local Authority warning me that at the expiry of the current licence it would be towed away and destroyed. They couldn't see what splendid little car it was despite being hand painted black and white, rather like a chess board.

I was taking no chances and brought it back before the fatal date. It romped through its MOT and I used it for another year. The Morris had done its job but was getting somewhat the worse for rot. I finally sold it to some young chaps for £50. Morris Minors were beginning to get really fashionable and I'm sure they thought they were getting a snip. I did too and was glad they were. At that time my daughter had had driving lessons and was getting near to her 21st birthday and it so happened that as I was driving back from Dorset I saw a shinning, black Morris Minor for sale. I went up to the house. It was owned by a real enthusiast but he had another Minor and couldn't keep both. We went for a drive in it and I felt that it was the most 'up together' Morris Minor I had ever been in, except for the new or nearly new ones. The idea that it would make a wonderful 21st birthday present flashed through my mind. Alice was just going on to Wye College in Kent after getting her degree in biology and ecology at the Royal Holloway College. She was a little uncertain about the idea of a Morris Minor at first but soon found her fellow students looking on it with considerable envy. She quickly passed her test in Ashford and it was a great step up from her Honda Scooter which been stolen.

My own motoring career was to be affected as usual by things on the side of the road. There was an Allegro for sale for only £150 in Fentiman Road, not a couple of hundred yards away from the house I'd bought in London. At the time this was a really good price for a car that was running well and had a reasonably long MOT. The Fiat was great for slipping in between buses and lorries, but wasn't really suitable for lugging about building materials and I knew that Allegros were not half as bad as the reputation which had been attached to them suggested, although I knew they were not as good as the early advertisements with dancing girls (a leg row) claimed. The present specimen not only had six months MOT but also a month's tax. After some discussion (not haggling) the owner let me have it for £135. I could drive it straight away so the Fiat went into mothballs, later to be sold to Howard Annette, the Secretary of the Austin Seven Owner's Club, exemplifying the fact that the principle Small is Beautiful applies to more than Austin Sevens.

A good roof rack and the Allegro was set up for the early part of my retirement. But it was not quite satisfactory. There was no back door and only a rotten little boot. I could carry rafters and sheets of corrugated iron but not electric cookers or nightstore heaters. That niggled but it was a vast improvement on the Fiat from that point of view, so I banished any thoughts of discontent from my mind, for the time being at least. The Allegro did a great job for about six months, during which time I covered about 10,000 miles with only one or two blips. I turned to John Kearley for the carburettor problems and for replacing one of the joined rubber brackets holding the rear sub-frame. You couldn't do that without having a special pump for setting up the hydrolastic suspension. Anyway the house was the overriding priority at that stage in my life. I was spending half the week in Southampton and half in London working on the house.

Quite by chance at this stage I visited some friends who lived near Milton Keynes. I knew one's father had been the Deputy Education Officer for Somerset and had bought her an extremely smart blue Mark II Allegro. I commented on how nice it was. 'Yes,' she said, 'It's just failed its MOT and wants more than it's worth spending on it. So it's on it way to the dump.' She showed me the horrible list of faults that the garage had concocted. I tried it and said I just didn't believe it and was told I could have it if I wanted it. After examining it more carefully I said I would take it down to Frank and if he passed it she could have it back. The main supposed fault was the suspension system which they said needed completely replacing (I think they just didn't understand hydrolastic suspension which needs pumping up occasionally) at some astronomical cost. I could see nothing. Neither could Frank and he was an expert on that system. It wanted a new tyre and a few minor things before it got its MOT. By this time my friends had bought a new car and simply didn't want it back.

The unfortunate side to this saga was that 'old faithful' got put on the back burner, a dirty old mustard coloured Allegro, in favour of a new – not quite new – shining blue model. In fact I put the old workhorse over in the Isle of Wight for the Summer and later prepared to put it in storage in to a friend's barn near Reading. A final drive across the Island to have tea with another friend in the ancient village of Nettlecombe resulted in the first blow to the poor overshadowed car's self-esteem. I parked it outside her cottage and when she came out to wave me goodbye it had been hit, my friend said, by a rather wild neighbour who used to tear up and down the lane in her very splendid 1960 Morris Minor. I thought it sacrilege that she should even have such a car, not without a touch of envy. The rear wing of the Allegro was badly dented. It didn't affect the driving but it did further dent my interest in the car and it was left to stand for five or six years. On top of that I had to take it out of the barn for a few months while an art exhibition was held there and during that time a considerable quantity of water found it way into the car and it stood there with flooded floor panes for a month or more. I knew that early Allegros had leaking problems and I was too lazy to cover it. When I did finally prepare to move it I found the wheels were locked and the callipers were seized. It seemed like a hopeless wreck but by one of those strange reversals of fate it suddenly became a prized historic car. The Allegro Club International had been formed and here was an Allegro that had survived – more or less – from the first year of production and that was very interesting indeed.

I had joined the club with the 'Blue Lady' and now her bedraggled, mustard coloured sister, in true Cinderella style was the one that would take the prizes for the earliest cars in many of the shows. I had spent quite a lot on the blue one and now decided to put it up for sale. It fetched £650 and I put the proceeds towards restoring her, by now more celebrated, sister. My hope was to get it up to the 30th birthday of the Allegro at the Heritage Museum in Gaydon in 2003. I had been in hospital in Dorset for over two months at the end of the previous year and had previously brought the car down to my friends at Tamarisk Farm so that Mervyn Langford could work on it and prepare it for its MOT. Mervyn had run a British Leyland garage for fifteen years and so had long experience with Allegros and, even more importantly, he didn't think they were nearly as bad as their reputation suggested.

I am running ahead of myself. Before I started using the Allegro I had a little blue Mini that John Kearley had looked after, so I knew it was good. I learned recently that John had been in charge of an aircraft engineering workshop which explained, I thought, the exceptional care he showed when dealing with cars. The Mini was great but it suffered from an almost non-existent boot and no back door. Perhaps I should have had a pick-up but that wouldn't really have done because at that stage I often carried more than one passenger. Slowly it became clear that the only solution would be a Metro despite the fact that sadly it didn't have the kind of reputation that the amazing Mini had accumulated. I found Minis running about in the most out of the way parts of the world. The French went mad about them. I even found them out in New Caledonia when I visited a friend there.

My opportunity came when I was visiting my friends in Dorset. Their son, Henry, came back from Bermuda where he had worked as a doctor for the authorities for several years. I remembered how when he was a young lad he had set about restoring a Morris Traveller at the farm. He had learned to weld and made a tremendously impressive and thorough job of it, but as the time when his medical studies required his full attention approached his interest in cars had to take a back seat. However it was never entirely extinguished and before he left for Bermuda he acquired a VW Beetle, the touring version, in pretty good condition. I started it up and ran it round the farm at fairly regular intervals while he was away. When the family came back his wife had a Metro for a time, which they decided to sell so we organised a part exchange with the blue Allegro. The only serious problem with the Metro was that it gobbled up oil. I had a choice. Either I sold it or I did something about the engine. I made some half-hearted attempts to sell it but as with most half-hearted things I failed. It so happened that just at that time Mervyn had a Metro engine which he had rebuilt for a customer who changed his mind and sold his car and so wanted to sell the engine also. I bought it for £100 and Mervyn fitted it. I soon had a rather excellent Metro which had the very special advantage of being one of the last of the 'baby' cars with the name Austin.

I spent quite a bit on overhauling the brakes, fitting new tyres, welding and everything needed to put it in first class condition. Just at that point another Morris Minor came in view – how sad I was that the Minor was not an Austin Minor! The sister of my friend in Nettlecombe, who lived at Newport in Staffordshire, had a superb 1968 Morris Minor, Trafalgar blue and in absolutely first rate condition. She loved the car but was forced by her disability to go round in a motorised wheelchair. She desperately wanted someone who would appreciate her beloved car to have it and insisted on offering it to me at only £200. How could I refuse? It had always been my ambition not to die driving a Morris Minor, that would have been inconsiderate to other road users, but to have one as my final car on the road, so long as I knew that the Austin Chummy was safely in the garage or in a museum like David Spence's Turnpike Centre on the Isle of Wight.

It was at just this point that a friend, Claudine Clee, who had been ill with cancer for many years, was finally taken into the Maudesley Hospital in Fulham. She had been given a Honda Civic and courageously learned to drive it at sixty. I went to visit her in hospital one evening when it was clear that she was near the end of her life. Her only son had just bought a new Peugeot and she said that the car would not be much use to him. 'If I leave it to you, will you use it?' I had to make a snap decision. It was an automatic with only 29,000 miles on the clock. I said, 'Yes,' and from that moment I felt honour bound to keep my promise. I didn't really like automatics, but I was later to learn, after a stroke when I had arm and leg trouble, that they did have their advantages. So at this point the line up was: one Austin Chummy, one 1938 Morris 8 Tourer (I think I'm past doing the work on it so suppose I must let it go), one Allegro, one Morris Minor and a Honda Civic, as well as a couple of Morris Minor wrecks.

Alice, my daughter, had seen John Kearley a few years ago about the Cavalier which she used to pull her horse box. He told me she said, 'I think Dad likes cars that are likely to go wrong'. There's a certain amount of truth in that and I have to admit it. I like things that can be repaired, not throw-away units. Perfection in a sense is slightly boring. Perhaps that was what was wrong with the Garden of Eden. But apart from that, I've spent my whole motoring life with manual changes and, in intense situations, one reverts to ingrained habits. Several times over the years I had the Honda I've put my foot on the accelerator when it was meant for the brake. Recently I parked on a bend with traffic coming fast both ways and not visible till the last moment. A builder's van was parked in front of me with something jutting out and, while I was in the shop another car parked very close behind me. My whole attention was concentrated on getting safely into the flow of traffic. I heard a crunch and immediately I realised what had happened. Not very much obvious damage was done but the radiator was penetrated. I vowed never to drive an automatic again. While it was being repaired down at Mervyn's I borrowed a friend's small Citroen AX. I loved both the gear change and the fact that it wasn't so difficult to keep within the speed limits with its little 950cc engine, and vowed that I'd return to my earlier dream of the

Morris Minor for the Summer and the Metro for the Winter months to save the former from being exposed to salty roads.

So that's where I stand 'motor car wise' as I bring this story to a close. I dream of the day: when mass produced cars will cease to flow off the production lines, when motor cars will only be made by engineers in their back yards, as they once were before the First World War, when aeroplanes in great numbers will cease to pollute the skies, when people will live and work within their own communities, when there is a fine public transport system, as there was before the Second World War, when people take their holidays once again in the English seaside towns or in our rural paradises, and visits to the other side of the world will be once or twice in a lifetime events, and when kings and presidents and prime ministers live as simply as their humblest subjects or citizens. I wonder if this is just an unrealistic dream or if the price of oil and oil products will slowly and inevitably rise and compel that dream to become a reality. We all know in the depths of our minds that things cannot go on as they are and that the alternative to my dream may be utter catastrophe for the whole of mankind.

Chapter 8

A Short Epilogue

In the real world, however, both our brightest dreams and our darkest fears are seldom, if ever, fully realized and I suppose this must apply to the future of the motor car also. Something between that I so ardently hoped for and the disaster I feared might engulf us, will surely emerge out of our present mess. A year or two ago I sat next to a gentleman who told me he'd just been over to Germany and had discovered that BMW were building the public transport systems for the major German cities and it so happened that one evening he found himself sitting beside the head of BMW at dinner, so he thought he's tackle the subject head on: 'I understood that BMW built motor cars and motorbikes, not public transport systems.' The reply he received was that cars in the future would only be for travelling between cities, not within them and that his company was simply adjusting to this new reality. That probably is the sort of thing that's going to happen and, if George Monbiot is correct, cars won't even be needed for the journeys between cities. At the Schumacher lectures in Bristol last year he told us that plans were being developed for coaches to go directly between the biggest cities, only stopping at points on the motorways to pick up passengers brought out by local buses from the nearby towns and cities, thereby avoiding wasting time driving into the town centres.

Road pricing is said to be seriously under consideration – if not already advanced beyond that stage – and in my opinion this is just about the worst of all possible worlds. Just imagine: if motorways cost £1.50 a mile and the lesser roads go down to 50p or less, all the minor roads will be clogged up with motorists desperate to cut excessive costs. Doing it the other way round, with motorways at 50p, the problem would merely be reversed. This is not to mention surveillance by satellites whose beady eyes would soon extend from our vehicles into our homes – all in the name of being able to catch criminals and terrorists. A revived version of Hitler's Gestapo would be justified on that basis. Let's hope that the Government will turn its attention in a different direction. Much as I dislike it I believe a substantial public transport levy on the cost of petrol (even as much as £1 a litre) will be necessary and it should go to a public body independent of Government, charged with extensive improvements in public transport. And all those commuters who complain so loudly about the present system should make it their business to watch it closely and make sure that it does its job and that the money is really well spent. In addition some sweeteners should be offered to motorists who opt to keep their cars on the road for special purposes, such as holidays when they take out the whole family or when they need to carry heavy objects. A public transport card similar to the Senior Citizen's Railcard and given free with their tax disc, could be one such benefit, allowing them to travel at greatly reduced rates or even free of charge. Another might be to cut the MOT to once every two years, since cars would be covering far fewer miles and there would be consequently far less wear and tear on their vital working parts.

One of the craziest ideas, it seems to me, is charging residents for street parking (which I would hope in the end would be abolished together snooping around every alleyway) with the armies of traffic wardens in cities on the basis of the emissions from their cars, since it merely transfers the source of pollution. I understand that the manufacture of a car causes more pollu-

tion than most cars create in their lifetime. It's fine for the manufacturers who are desperate to sell their cars, but surely it
would be much better if they took a leaf out of BMW's book and
turned their hand to public transport instead. But in any case
pollution would be automatically reduced substantially in a
meaningful way if the number of cars on the road were to be sig-
nificantly cut because of the price of fuel. I know it's not a
pleasant prospect but I fear that the alternatives are worse.

The few people, who have deliberately given up their cars or
opted for a partnership scheme, find a sense of relief from the
tyranny of the motor car. They have found that instead of
serving them the car was actually dominating the pattern of
their lives. Many of us need to see much more clearly the way
ring roads and one-way systems make our town and cities far
less pleasant places than they once were when only the odd car
pottered around at leisurely, human speeds. And now I see that
Ken Livingstone is seriously thinking of imposing a 20mph
speed limit on the whole of London. We probably need it but I
don't want it imposed, especially on people with a 90 mile an
hour mindset. The mindset needs changing first or I fear it may
cause chaos.

The one worry I have about the fuel levy is that it will hit
country people rather hard. I know how dependent they have
been forced to become on their cars, particularly since the bus
services to outlying parts have been so severely axed. Some real
lateral thinking about this problem will be urgently called for.
Maybe in the first place they might be given some relief from the
fuel levy. Most country people, could with some judicious
thought, reduce the number of journeys they make. Giving their
neighbours lifts and partnership schemes, perhaps with small
minibuses might also help greatly and even more could be done
if the regulations that rightly apply to the bigger public transport companies, were relaxed for small firms to run minibuses.
But even the application of the fuel levy to country dwellers is
not all doom and gloom. It could help to revive the spirit of the

old countryside communities and that in itself would be a big plus.

All in all I think the petrol option is the best one and let's cut out all unnecessary journeys and let's save up our money to really enjoy our motoring on special occasions, like Mr Josiah Oldcastle. Our vintage and classic care enthusiasts can point to the secret of convivial motoring. A few billionaires may continue to run about in their vehicles – probably 4 X 4's – but they'll miss out on that secret.

Appendix 1

A Tale of Two Allegros

John Coleman

The following article appeared in the Christmas 2006 issue of
Quartic, *the journal of the Allegro Club International.*

In fact it is about the four Allegros I have owned. The story of
how Allegros came into my life has some interesting and
unusual sides to it. At the time of the Referendum on member-
ship of the Common Market in 1975 I was on the anti-Market
side although I always had a great liking for the countries of the
Continent and in the 50's I'd been on a couple of long trips
round Europe in my 1934 Morris tourer: one to northern
Europe going up into Scandinavia and the other going into
southern Germany, Switzerland, touching Italy and back again
through France. I was driving an excellent Volvo 144S which my
friend Dr. Michael Goldacre always referred to as my 'millionaire's car', the only plutocratic car I've ever owned. Because of
the stickers I had in my rear window someone put a note under
my windscreen wiper to the effect that why didn't I have a
British car? I don't think it was quite so polite as that but it
touched a nerve and so I thought I'd better do something about

it. As Allegros had fairly recently come out and as I had always, like my father, been a fan of Austins I thought I would look for one. I spoke to the deputy head of the school at which I taught because I knew his son had a garage, 'Go and see David,' he said, so I did. He had been briefed about my arrival and said, 'You don't want an Allegro.' 'Yes I do,' I replied. After some discussion, he finally responded, 'Well, if you insist I suppose I must get you one,' and he did, an M reg 1300 in Harvest Gold, the same as the one I have now but I suspect that if the exact time of manufacture had been established it would have qualified as tax exempt. It was a come-down after the Volvo but I got used to it and quite liked everything about it except the square steering wheel, which I believe had a lot to do with the early growth of its unfortunate and unfair reputation. In addition I felt more comfortable myself. Nobody could accuse me of being unpatriotic now and I got quite good service out of it for a year, but I hankered after a later one, so I went to see David again. 'I've got the very thing for you, a demonstration model that's like new.' As it was only a few months old and was well below the new price, I thought I'd have a look. It was a horrible sickly lime/yellow colour, which nearly put me off but I told myself not to be daft about the colour. Maybe it will turn out to be an excellent motor. At the time I had just bought a house in London, which was in fact an old off licence and I was busy trying to turn it into my new home. I collected doors and rafters and knockers and lovely brass locks from skips around the country. You could do that then. I'd had one problem with the car soon after I'd bought it. The alternator packed up. I got that sorted out. I'd got such a good bargain from David that I couldn't go back to him and so I had to fork out for a new alternator. In spite of being a little put out by that I said to myself, 'I can't blame the car for the alternator any more than I would say it was a rotten car because one of the tyres was faulty'. It was a wonderful workhorse for a couple of years. I clocked up 120,000 miles and I began to form a very high opinion of it. However I began to get rather short of money which I needed for my London house. I had an old and very tatty Morris Minor in my back garden, which I'd bought for £20, so regretfully I thought I'd sell the Allegro and resurrect the decrepit old Minor – nobody valued them then unless they were in first class condition. I advertised the Allegro and had several phone calls. A chap from South London came over with an engineer to test it out and advise him on it – to run it down, I thought. But no, he was clearly impressed and I heard later that he gave it a very good report, with the result that I sold it for almost the same price I'd paid for it a couple of years and 120,000 miles earlier. I was sad to see it go, but it left me with a very good impression of Allegros and I learned to take no notice of the nonsense that was going around about them.

The Minor made a brave job of doing what I expected of it but rust was really beginning to get the better of it. So one day a year or two later when I as walking down the road near my house in Vauxhall I saw an Allegro for sale for £150, an extremely reasonable price in the early eighties. I rang up about it and met the owner at the roadside and he agreed to let me have it for £135. I still have the receipt written on a piece of an old paper towel. After a good run in it I was satisfied it would serve my immediate needs. It was a 1300 and Harvest Gold – dirty mustard I called it then – like my very first one. I used it for a couple of years and it ran well apart from the usual minor things: a rear subframe bracket, new callipers – the most expensive item – and tyres etc.

I hit on a couple of very nice Morris Minors which I ran for a time and enjoyed in turn and then sold for a very handsome profit. The poor old 'mustard' Allegro had done a good job and I knew I'd get next to nothing for it, so I kept it in a friend's barn in the country with the good feeling that I had a good car put aside for a rainy day! I did turn the engine over occasionally but I didn't look after it as I should have done. In the meantime I visited some friends in Milton Keynes who I knew had a lovely shining blue Allegro which her father had bought for her as a second car.

I was dumbfounded when they told me that it had failed its
MOT and the garage had told them that amongst a long list of
things that needed doing to it was the replacement of the whole
of the hydrolastic system. I was sure it was a load of rubbish and
wasted no time before getting underneath it and having a good
look. 'You can have it,' they said and I replied I'd take it down to
my man in London, who I knew would give an honest opinion.
Apart from a few minor things it sailed through its MOT, as I
thought it would.

I took it back to them but in the meantime they bought
another car and insisted I should keep it. This was when I made
my first acquaintance with the Allegro Club. I came to meetings
and noticed on several occasions that if I'd had the earlier model
I'd have walked away with the prize for the earliest Allegro there.
One day I thought I must get it on the road again. In the end I
decided to sell the blue one, which I did and got the princely
sum of £650 for it, all of which I spent on the hopeful prize-
winner. In spite of being neglected the engine was still running
well and it seemed worth lashing out the proceeds from my
previous sale on the early model. It had had a nasty knock on the
offside rear wing from the last day I had it on the Isle of Wight
and the brakes were seized up. I was getting a bit old myself and
didn't feel up to tackling it, so I took it down to my friends' farm
in Dorset and from there to Mervyn who had a small workshop
in Melklash and who had been the works manager of a BMC
agency for 15 years and knew Allegros inside and out as well as
having a fair opinion of them.

To cut a longer story short the outcome of all this was that I
was able to take it up to Longbridge for the Austin Motor
Company Centenary in 2005. I went up first to my son in
Stafford. Coming back down I left the M5 motorway for
Longbridge and just as I did so I saw a man waving trade plates
at the side of the road. It turned out that he had worked at the
factory. He not only directed me to my destination, but gave me
some useful hints and when we stopped we looked under the

bonnet together and he saw the black underseal sprayed on almost everything. This was one of the few that were done in the factory, he explained, that's why the underneath has lasted without welding. I knew the floor panels were remarkably original and now I knew why. I was slightly irritated that it didn't receive the appreciation that was lavished on those that had been brought up to concours condition.

Well, that's my story except for one little incident on my way back to Southampton, where I now keep the car. I called in to see a retired friend in Winchester – we oldies get together – who had been Transmission Controller of Southern Television, that's the person who sees that the programmes fit together and that the adverts are appropriate; 'Oh, I remember them' he said, 'Do you remember the early ads with a row of dancing girls doing the can-can?' **A LEG ROW**

Appendix 2

A Statistic

*The following is an article which appeared in the **Guardian** many years ago when it was based in Manchester and it so impressed the licensing authorities that they sent a copy out with every driving licence.*

You have driven this car along this road many times without incident. It is dark, but the road surface is good and visibility is all right. You are relaxed. The car purrs along superbly because it is a superb car and you are a bit inclined to brag about it to your friends but you are not a fast driver by nature, and really it is a bit wasted on you because you've never had it flat out and you never will, and you're not really the type who has to be first away from the lights or bust. None the less, you're fond of it and proud of it, and proud of the Institute of Advanced Motorists badge on the front. And you haven't even bothered to insure it except for third party because you've been driving for years and you've never so much as scraped an eighth of an inch of paint off any vehicle in your life, and it takes two to make a crash, and you don't ever intend to be the other one. That's the sort of person you are and the sort of car you're in at 10.15 that night. You are travelling at 32 miles per hour, and you know the chap in front is travelling at 32mph as well because you've been following him for a long time and he's a good driver. You note that almost subconsciously because you've done a lot of advanced driving training and they teach you to note everything, and particularly to note the driving behaviour of other vehicles. He's a long way in front, because you never follow anything closely, because that's something else they were hot about in training. You could have passed him half a dozen times if you'd wanted to but what's the point? There's no hurry.

He indicates his intention of turning right up a little road that no one ever goes up anyway and you wonder idly what he's going there for. His right flasher is flashing he pulls to the crown of the road, and he practically stops to let through a southbound vehicle. You are now approaching what the police driving manual refers to as a "Hazard." Ahead is the main road approaching the brow of a hill and bending left. A junction on the right. A car centrally placed about to turn right. The response is causal, relaxed, automatic. Foot off the gas. Cover the brake. Slight reduction in speed. Pull in left to clear the centre car. Total attention on driving. Watch the bend. Watch the hill. Watch the other driver. Note road works on left. Still quite a way to go before you actually pass him, but watch it. He might pull back in front of you. Perfect control. Perfect confidence. Recognition of "Hazard" correctly allowed for. No danger.

Someone else on the road. Southbound vehicle coming towards you round the bend and over the hill. Crikey, he's shifting! But no danger, ample room for all three of us. But what's happening? That chap in the middle of the road is moving off. He's turning. He can't be, but he is.

Please, God, it can't be happening. It can't be true. They're going to hit.

"Foot off the gas, cover the brake," they'd said through all those months of training. So the brakes are already covered and those discs are earning their keep. The only emergency stop in a lifetime. And a stop so fast and so vicious that the imprint of the steering wheel is found in bruises on the body next morning.

But even now it isn't your accident. Not yet. You've only stopped short because you know those two must hit and you are aiming to stay clear of that shambles. You have time to think. You have time to realise that they are going to hit and they will hit very hard, that you are the only one there to see what must be done and you are afraid. You are afraid of corpses and twisted metal and a steering column through the body and out of the back, and blood. You have time to be afraid of all that while they are busy hitting each other and your magnificent bit of machinery has brought itself to a dead stop, and far faster than any figures on the back of the Highway Code because these are discs in superb condition, and a good road, and four new tyres.

They do hit. You've underestimated the speed of the south-bound vehicle. It goes head-on into the side of the car across its path, but that doesn't stop it. It doesn't even seem to slow it. It's coming on. It's out of control. It isn't even coming straight. It's crabwise and deformed, and as though some gigantic demon had picked it up and flung it, and it's coming for you- more or less. Your engine is still running. You've still got time. Your brain is still functioning. Left hand ditch? Can't. Roadworks. Swerve, scattered bodies over there, anyway. Can't see because it's dark. Back? Only hope. Reduce impact. Instinct to glance in mirror. Nothing behind. Slam into reverse. Please miss. He must be still doing fifty. Clutch in. just moving back. Reduce impact. Please, God, NO!

Everyone has stopped. There are two people in your car now. There's you, at the wheel; and there's you looking at you at the wheel. It's a funny sensation. You, at the wheel, you're a washout. You're in pain. You've never known such pain in all your life before. And you're moaning. Rather like a kitten, you're moaning with quite regular mewing sounds. You're in a funny sort of position- you at the wheel, sort of twisted up. And you're not doing anything about it. You're just sitting there moaning. You, standing looking at you at the wheel, you're in better shape. You're saying: "You've been in a crash, and you're probably the only person still alive. This is a main road, and other traffic will be coming along soon. That car on your bows has steam or smoke coming from under the bonnet. It is going to catch fire any second, and there are people in that car. You have to get out. It doesn't matter how much you're hurt. You've got to get out. You've got to stop the traffic. You've got to see if there's anyone alive in there, and if there is, you've got to get them out."

The second you win and you find that you can get out, and you can walk. And the amazing thing is, there's a chap getting out of the car on your bonnet, and he can walk, too, but he's all over bloody. And dirty. And he's clawing at his front passenger door because he's seen the smoke, too. So you leave that to him, and you just concentrate on stopping the traffic, and you walk down the road towards a car. You're right in the middle of the road, and if he doesn't see you, or if he isn't quick enough off the mark, you're a goner but you wave both hands at him and he stops. And you say: "Please, there's been a terrible smash. It's just happened. You're the first here. There's people hurt. Killed, I think. Please go back and get an ambulance and the police. Please be quick." But he doesn't take it in. He wants to know what's happened, and whether there's room to turn round, and his window's jammed, and he's useless. But there's something else coming now, a heavy lorry. Sense from a lorry driver. Healthy young man away at the double, and you go back.

And now the bloody young man is lifting a young girl from the wreckage and laying her on the verge among the roadworks. She is even bloodier than he is. You've still got one headlamp working, and that is the only light on the scene. You can see the blood quite clearly by the light of that lamp. She is writhing a bit on the verge, in an attitude of complete abandonment and inde- cency. Then she lies quite still and he covers her. You know she is dead. You wonder about the other car, but the young man is walking over there, and you leave it to him again. Anyway, it's dark over there and you're such a coward you don't want to go and look. You excuse yourself by thinking that as you know no first aid you could serve no useful purpose. So you stand beside what is left of your car, and you wait, and you don't look at the girl. And you don't really think about anything at all. You are not even in very great pain any more, but you know you've got to look at your right leg, because that's where the pain was, and you use the headlight to look, and it's all bloody and un-real looking. That's YOUR leg. It's always been all right in the past. Best not look any more. That blood will just go away if you leave it. Anyway, why stay here? What to do now? If you go away, you'll be in trouble for failing to report an accident. If you stay, you'll just see more horrible things when they uncover whatever is in that other car. You can report the accident tomorrow. Yes, that's right. Walk home now, and report the accident tomorrow. Forget about the car. Don't want that any more. Home is 15 miles away, but it doesn't matter. Just go home, and maybe tomorrow it won't have happened. That's right, down the hill, quite easy going. Leg doesn't really mind being walked on at all. But the thrillers are wrong when they talk of warm blood trickling down. It isn't warm; it's cold. Everything is cold. There isn't a footpath to walk on, but it doesn't matter. Just walk in the middle of the road. Walk home. Police car pulling up? Failing to report an accident? It's an offence. You know it is. But they seem to know all about it. They want to know what car you were in, but you can't remember the number. They put you in their own car. Riding in a police car indeed. Proper Z car, with radio. They are using the radio. Hold the ambulance. Fifth casualty found. Leg injuries and shock. Funny, they don't seem to mind that you didn't report the accident. They don't even seem to want a driving licence. Just as well. Left it at home. Then you're in the ambulance. And now you resist. Now you really resist. You're not going anywhere with that lot. Not with the girl who's dead, and the boy who's so dirty and bloody, and goodness knows what from the other car.

But they win. The police and the ambulance men are stronger than you are, and they neither know nor care that you are abject with terror all over again at seeing what was in that smash. But you do see it. You can't put it off any longer. You sit on a seat and you realise that this is a new experience. For the first time in your life you are in an ambulance in a hurry. Lamps flashing, horns blowing, passing everything in sight. Wrong side of the road half the time. Magnificent driver. You have time to appreciate that. Beautiful driving, and everyone melting out of your road. The ambulance man explains that you are going straight to the city. Nearly 20 miles to go, but serious injuries aboard, and better to go straight to large teaching hospital. Moving very fast, but very smooth. Young girl is lying on stretcher covered in blankets, face and head covered with blood-stained bandages. Blood is very light, bright sort of red, not the sort of colour you squeeze a drop of out of your finger. Apparently she's not dead, just very seriously injured. You know that, because the ambulance driver has radio as well, and he's telling the hospital all about all of you.

The boy who is so dirty and so bloody looks at you and says, "Were you driving the second car I hit?" You say "Yes." You want to add "But what the hell were you going at that speed for?", but you don't, because he has his arms around the girl who will soon be dead. And you look at the other chap – the good steady driver, the one you followed for miles, the one who made an atrocious error of judgment. You can't see much of him because of the bandages, but he doesn't say anything at all, though his eyes are open. The ambulance attendant tries to talk to him but he doesn't answer, and the attendant tells the driver he doesn't like the look of him, and his head's in a mess, and for God's sake get a move on. You try not to look to your left. She is a middle-aged woman and there is so much blood on her you cannot even tell where she is hurt. Why is the blood such a very light, bright red? She is being sick; she is very, very sick.

She goes on vomiting. And when she is not vomiting she is apologising, to you, and to the ambulance attendant, because you are being splashed with blood, or vomit, or whatever it is, and she is ashamed, and apologetic, and hurt, and helpless. And the attendant says, "For God's sake get on with it Tom. We've got a right load here." And Tom says, "Oh, shut up!" And you say nothing.

The next day you are two lines in the national press, and for about four days you are a paragraph in the local press. And now you are just statistics in the Road Accidents Report, 1963.

Reprinted from The Guardian

It is well worth reading again and again. It reflects the principles of The Institute of Advanced Motorists, of which I am a member, and I am convinced that its disciplines have been invaluable in old age; reading the roads, good observation, setting a good course and all the things that the writer includes in his article. Older drivers of older cars know how important it used to be to anticipate hazards. Herbert Austin answered these critics of the brakes on his cars saying, 'Good brakes make bad drivers.' I have done my best to encourage meeting between the Institute of Advanced Motorists and classic and vintage car clubs. The latter have something important to add to advanced drivers' message. Like Mr. Oldcastle they drive for fun and not because of the pressures of modern life. And we could all take to heart the message from Peter Rodger on Eco Driving. The first hint- leave your car at home!

Advanced Driving, Winter 2006

We can create a better world by driving less and when we drive by driving well.

Index

Also available from New European Publications

CHILDSCOURT

John Coleman

Foreword by Nigel Whiskin MBE

ISBN 1-872410-46-4

149 pages • Paperback £11.95

First published in 1967, this book is still very relevant today as it discusses the work and theories of Bill Malcolm's innovative approach to teaching and discipline in schools. Malcolm believed that democratic self-government created the best environment for learning. The school was closed recently due to Government views on Special Education.

"Interesting points that emerge are his suspicion of too much reliance on the psychiatrist and the way he has won the co-operation and admiration of the local authorities who send him pupils."
Times Literary Supplement

FROUDE TODAY

John Coleman

ISBN 1-872410-38-3

Paperback £12.95 • Hardback £21.00

One of our great somewhat misunderstood historians whose ideas on religion, science, education and even empire that he regarded as a network of different peoples rather than a centralised organization, are as germane to today's problems as they were in Froude's own times. His research examines the motives of the most powerful players in the Europe of the sixteenth century and points to a way of understanding power in all ages.

THE CONSCIENCE OF EUROPE
Edited by John Coleman

ISBN 9-287140-30-8

212 pages • Paperback £12.00

Published by the Council of Europe in association with New European Publications

The Council of Europe is the institution through which the spiritual and moral leadership of Europe should be expressed. Contributors include: Cosmo Russell, Vaclav Havel, Peter Smithers and George Carey.

"The approach to the subject is decidedly spiritual, as befits an examination of conscience, and provides a welcome change from the usual economic or political analyses of the EU…"
Alain Woodrow, *The Tablet*.

"Churchmen and statesmen, poets and philosophers, each was asked to contribute a response which might be collated, with the original essay, into a compiled work. The result is truly remarkable – and in truth impossible to review."
James Bourlet, Britain and Overseas (Economic Research Council).

"The conscience of Europe is a book for both eurosceptics and europhiles. As such I recommend it highly as a means of stimulating the woefully inadequate discussion in Britain about the future of Europe."
Graham Dines, *East Anglia Daily Times*.

GLOBAL FLYER
Brian Milton

ISBN 1-872410-36-7

229 pages • Paperback £10.95

In 1998 Brian Milton and fellow pilot Keith Reynolds, who abandoned the flight, attempted to fly a single-engine micro light around the world in eighty days. Their flight aboard GT Global Flyer retraces as far as possible the route taken by Phileas Fogg in Jules Verne's classic story. They flew what is virtually no more than a hang glider with a motorbike slung underneath, the smallest and lightest aircraft ever to attempt such a hazardous journey. Leaving London and passing over Europe, Milton and Reynolds flew to the Middle East and onwards through China, Japan and into Russia. Crossing the Pacific, they reached Alaska and flew through Canada and the USA, before going to Greenland and Iceland, then Scotland and finally back to London.

Global Flyer is Brian Milton's account of this incredible journey and of the hazards and dangers which he and Reynolds had to overcome – ranging from engine failure and atrocious weather conditions to being shot at by Syrian fighters.

This is a story of flying in the face of adversity, of a constant battle against time and the elements and of overcoming obstacles and challenges that even Phileas Fogg did not have to contend with.

"...Global Flyer around the world in 80 days was without doubt the most extraordinary flight of this century."
Dick Smith, publisher and founder of *Australian Geographic.*

COLEMAN'S DRIVE
John Coleman

ISBN 1-872410-06-5

260 pages plus illustrations

Paperback **£10.00**

This is the true story of a ride from Buenos Aires to New York in a 1925 Austin 7 *Chummy,* through the mountains, deserts and jungles of South and Central America.

"Coleman's Drive with its implied challenge to a classic of travel is, like its author, tough, cool and daring."

"His fantastic journey had to be improvised in short stretches of guesswork on the edge of risk."
Times Literary Supplement

"Coleman's book is a fascinating account of a fascinating journey."
The Guardian

"This is one of the best travel books of recent times."
Motor Sport

CHASING GHOSTS

An Attempt at the Atlantic by Microlight

Brian Milton

ISBN 1-8724102-3-5

224 pages • Hardback £16.99

The ghosts are the British pilots Alcock and Brown, and Charles Lindbergh who in 1919 and 1927 flew non-stop from America to Europe. This is the story of Milton's attempt to follow these great aviators in a tiny microlight, an aircraft no bigger than a large kite.

"...This is a story about a man and the people around him. I won't say that the flying is incidental, but Brian's generous revelations of his own fears, struggles and heroes fill this book with delight after delight for anyone who loves the air."
Noel Whittall, Editor *XC Magazine*.

"Here is an adventure story, the fourth world class adventure from one of the world's last remaining adventurers, Brian Milton."
Jack McCornack, *Ultralight Flying*, USA.

AN ENGLISH AMATEUR IN ANTARCTICA

Brian Milton

ISBN 1-872410-43-X

208 pages, including 64 colour photo pages

Hardback £19.95

In December 2003, to mark his fiftieth birthday, Martin Burton took an aeroplane to the South Pole and skied out of the Antarctic, 700 miles to Hercules Inlet, the nearest sea ice. Burton, a successful financial trader in the City of London, took two companions, Polar veteran Geoff Somers MBE as navigator, and young Norwegian ski sailing expert Ronny Finsass as his guest. In temperatures as low as 38 below zero, over frozen surfaces rough enough to destroy all three of the expedition's sledges, it was not an easy journey. An English Amateur in Antarctica traces the origins of Burton's ambition, reaching back to a youth of 17 with long hair and a motorbike torn between travelling the world and the "smell of money". This honest story of an amateur adventurer owes nothing to sponsors or other patrons, as Burton overcomes numerous setbacks to achieve his ambition.